LeeRay M. Costa
Andrew J. Matzner

Male Bodies, Women's Souls
Personal Narratives of Thailand's Transgendered Youth

Pre-publication
REVIEWS,
COMMENTARIES,
EVALUATIONS . . .

Male Bodies, Women's Souls
Personal Narratives of Thailand's Transgendered Youth

THE HAWORTH PRESS
Human Sexuality
Eli Coleman, PhD
Editor

Tongzhi: Politics of Same-Sex Eroticism in Chinese Societies by Chou Wah-shan

Sexuality and Gender in Postcommunitst Eastern Europe and Russia edited by Aleksandar Štulhofer and Theo Sandfort

Head Over Heels: Wives Who Stay with Cross-Dressers and Transsexuals by Virginia Erhardt

Male Bodies, Women's Souls: Personal Narratives of Thailand's Transgendered Youth by LeeRay M. Costa and Andrew J. Matzner

Male Bodies, Women's Souls
Personal Narratives of Thailand's Transgendered Youth

LeeRay M. Costa
Andrew J. Matzner

The Haworth Press®
New York • London • Oxford

For more information on this book or to order, visit
http://www.haworthpress.com/store/product.asp?sku=5750

or call 1-800-HAWORTH (800-429-6784) in the United States and Canada
or (607) 722-5857 outside the United States and Canada

or contact orders@HaworthPress.com

The Haworth Press, Inc., 10 Alice Street, Binghamton, NY 13904-1580.

PUBLISHER'S NOTE
The development, preparation, and publication of this work has been undertaken with great care. However, the Publisher, employees, editors, and agents of The Haworth Press are not responsible for any errors contained herein or for consequences that may ensue from use of materials or information contained in this work. The Haworth Press is committed to the dissemination of ideas and information according to the highest standards of intellectual freedom and the free exchange of ideas. Statements made and opinions expressed in this publication do not necessarily reflect the views of the Publisher, Directors, management, or staff of The Haworth Press, Inc., or an endorsement by them.

Identities and circumstances of individuals discussed in this book have been changed to protect confidentiality.

Cover design by Marylouise E. Doyle.

Library of Congress Cataloging-in-Publication Data

Costa, LeeRay M.
    Male bodies, women's souls : personal narratives of Thailand's transgendered youth / LeeRay M. Costa, Andrew J. Matzner.
        p. cm.
    Includes bibliographical references and index.
    ISBN: 978-0-7890-3114-3 (case : alk. paper)
    ISBN: 978-0-7890-3115-0 (soft : alk. paper)
    1. Transsexuals—Thailand. 2. Transsexualism—Thailand. 3. Youth—Sexual behavior—Thailand. I. Matzner, Andrew. II. Title.

    HQ77.95.T5C67 2007
    306.76'8083509593—dc22
                                                                                    2006022967

CONTENTS

Foreword

OVERVIEW

LeeRay Costa and Andrew Matzner have made a significant contribution to the study of gender variance in Thailand. The authors offer a refreshing view of the *"kathoey"* (reframed as *sao braphet song*) through the lens of a reflexive anthropology moored to feminism and humanism and presented through the narrative genre. This book represents a relatively recent venue in anthropological studies of gender variance, one in which Matzner is on the forefront through his prior publication of narratives of Hawaiian *mahu* and male-to-female transgendered people (Matzner, 2001).

Male Bodies, Women's Souls offers a unique approach in that the narrative accounts are based on a textual rather than oral historical rendering. Twelve Chiang Mai University transgendered students (referred to as *sao braphet song*) were each asked to write an essay (one to ten pages in length) about their experiences with the goal of educating others about their lives as transgendered people in Thai society. Two additional narratives focusing on Rosepaper, a Chiang Mai University club for *sao braphet song,* were included, expanding the context for situating the twelve personal narratives. Two other reflections further augment the framework for interpreting the *sao braphet song* narratives. Mumu, a very open *sao braphet song* CMU cafeteria worker and Aom, a university woman who interviewed three *sao braphet song* friends, offer alternative perspectives that complicate simplistic renderings of gender variance and provide a textual terrain for comparison.

Costa and Matzner's *Male Bodies, Women's Souls* is a valuable and much needed addition to the field of transgender studies, filling a gap in the literature for narrative voices. Although the book has much to recommend, for example, Chapter 2, "Gender and Sexuality in Thailand," contains an excellent critical review of the literature on the

Male Bodies, Women's Souls
© 2007 by The Haworth Press, Inc. All rights reserved.
doi:10.1300/5750_a

kathoey and on Thai gender ideologies, for the purpose of this Foreword I would like to limit my discussion to five particularly prominent contributions to Thai transgender studies. These include: (1) clarifying the terminology regarding Thai *Sao Braphet Song* (i.e., *kathoey*), (2) attention to issues of the power differential between researcher and researched, (3) dispelling a legacy that Thai society is extremely tolerant of the *kathoey* as a third gender, (4) destabilizing totalizing views of gender identity and complicating Thai gendered categories of *gay* and *sao braphet song,* and (5) demonstrating the value of the narrative approach and offering a heuristic tool for future research.

CLARIFYING THE TERMINOLOGY

The first page sets the tone for the respect and compassion that Costa and Matzner have for their *sao braphet song* participants. This infuses the entire book from the discussion of methods, to the reflexive and strategic incorporation of the narratives, through to the authors' thematic interrogation in Chapter 5, "Analyzing *Sao Braphet Song* Narratives." A number of scholars who have theorized gender variance have inherited the Thai *"kathoey"* as Thailand's unofficial "third gender." Into this fray, Costa and Matzner have complicated such a notion, offering a glimpse of the ambiguity that circumscribes the term *kathoey* for both the Thai people and scholars alike, including reference to "gay" men, "transvestites," "transsexuals," and "drag queens." Indeed, Costa and Matzner challenge the currently popular usage of *"kathoey"* and propose instead the appellation *sao braphet song* as one preferred by their transgendered participants. This keen sense of sensitivity and knowledge comes not only from the authors' narrative research project but from their general ethnographic wherewithal based on extended stays in Thailand from 1997 to 1999, returning again for four months in 2000, and on their fluency in the Thai language both written and spoken. *Sao braphet song* was thus selected not only because of its preference by the participants but because a nuanced understanding of the Thai language suggested ambiguous and negative connotations ascribed to the word *kathoey,* for example, it is more polite to use *sao braphet song.*

THE POWER DIFFERENTIAL
BETWEEN THE RESEARCHER
AND THE RESEARCHED

The authors have taken seriously anthropology's "post-modern turn" with its call for attention to the potential colonizing relations among researchers and their "subjects" (Mascia-Lees and Black, 2000: 92-94; Brightman, 1995: 511-526). Whereas anthropologists in the past discussed "informants" and research populations, reflexive and dialogical anthropology takes a more commensurate stance on these relations. Informants have become "consultants" and "participants" in an effort to divest anthropology of the inequalities inherent in researcher and subject relations (Skomal, 1994: 4). According to Abu-Lughod (1991: 142), this was in part spawned by the work of indigenous anthropologists and ethnic and feminist anthropologists "not just because they position themselves with reference to two communities but because when they present the 'Other' they are presenting themselves, [and consequently] they speak with a complex awareness of and investment in reception" (in Bolin and Granskog, 2003).

Costa and Matzner have genuinely engaged in a collaborative effort. They are extremely attentive to positioning themselves as horizontally as is possible vis-à-vis the *sao braphet song* with whom they worked. Throughout they refer to *sao braphet song* as "participants," "narrators," and "storytellers," and themselves as "researchers," "listeners," and "interpreters." Theirs is a concerted and radical effort to destabilize the hierarchical power relations that come with Western socioeconomic status and education. A variety of techniques are utilized by the authors to achieve this, including transparency. For example, Costa and Matzner discuss the structural limitations on absolute parity that come with their "authorial" privilege and access to the means of publication. Although the final chapter (Chapter 5 "Analyzing *Sao Braphet Song* Narratives") offers a discussion of common themes found among the narrators, the authors go to great lengths to explain that this chapter should not be considered a "conventional conclusion" in which the authors' co-opt the voices of the narrators with their anthropological authority and voice-over. Their goals are honorable in that the vestigial asymmetry in their positioning as Western gender-normative researchers provides them the opportunity and resources to publish the stories and voices of their *sao braphet song* participants.

DISPELLING THAI TOLERANCE

Costa and Matzner offer an in-depth discussion and analysis of social attitudes toward *sao braphet song* spanning various discourses, from the popular media through the academic. Thai popular discourses reflect positive attributes regarding *sao braphet song* beauty and talent in the expressive careers and arts. Tourist commentary touts the tolerance and acceptance of gender diversity in Thailand, emphasizing "exotic otherness" and *"kathoey"* roles as sex workers. The authors note that some researchers have emphasized this view of tolerance (e.g., Morris, 1994), while others have noted the increasing stigmatization and social subordination facing Thai transgendered persons (Matzner, 2001; Nanda, 2000: 77-78). However, what is missing from the literature are the voices of *sao braphet song,* whose narratives paint a vivid picture of the opprobrium and discrimination they have faced, including physical violence, familial intolerance, and social rejection. Such accounts subvert popular and scholarly accounts of Thai indulgence and magnanimity toward *sao braphet song.* The narratives in *Male Bodies, Women's Souls* are all the more telling since the participants were not asked specifically to address the issue of acceptance but rather were given general directions to write essays that would educate people about themselves as *sao braphet song.* Their voices speak out as individuals rather than as categories of people, alerting their audience to their suffering and their desire for acceptance and valuing as contributing members of Thai society.

PREVIOUS RESEARCH

In order for me to address the significance of Costa and Matzner's *sao braphet song* narratives to the study of gendered identities and ideologies of gender, I hope you will forgive a brief digression into the history of anthropological and scholarly research into the subject of gender-variant identities. This digression will better situate the unique contribution of the narrative voices of *sao braphet song* to this endeavor.

Researchers have theorized gender, sex, and sexuality in diverse ways throughout the history of gender and sexuality studies. Over the past thirty years scholarly efforts have been directed at uncoupling gender as a sociocultural construct from the male and female biological and physiological bodies. Kessler and McKenna (1978) were among the first to really explore and promote social constructionism with reference to transsexual persons, giving impetus to a vanguard of subsequent researchers who critiqued gender binarism with reference to Western transsexuals and transgendered people. The ethnographic record provided ample evidence of gender variant persons, and ethnographic research in the early days documented ample evidence of the *"berdache,"* subsequently referred to as two-spirits (Jacobs, 1994: 7; Bolin, 1996: 27-30). An impressive literature on gender variance has burgeoned over the past thirty years. This was buttressed by research that "nature" (read: biology) was no more binary than culture, offering a plethora of "sexual" possibilities and blendings, including the chromosomal and hormonal, e.g., Money and Ehrhardt's (1972) research on hermaphrodites and Fausto-Sterling's (2000) discussion of the five sexes. The simple and essentialist binarism of male and female, woman and man embedding Western notions of the genders was challenged by a global record of multiple genders, gender variance, and the deconstruction of gendered paradigms by ethnographers.

Anthropologists have happily documented gender variance cross-culturally. A plethora of synonyms—including two-spirits (Jacobs, 1994: 7), supernumerary genders (Martin and Voorhies, 1975), third sexes (Herdt, 1994), gender liminality (Besnier, 1994), and beyond such as "not men" (Kulick, 1997)—were invented as the term *berdache* fell into disfavor as ethnocentric and inaccurate. The world became a many-gendered thing in the years since anthropologists first made reference to gender variance (Bolin, 2004).

Anthropological studies of gender variance were important in addressing issues of ethnocentrism and were embraced early on by an emergent transsexual and transgendered community in legitimizing their position and arguing for tolerance in the 1970s and 1980s (Bolin, 1988). Concomitantly, the emergence of the transsexual identity in North America and Europe as a discrete social identity tied to the possibility of hormonal and surgical alterations, accelerated gender variance research, and encouraged the theorizing of gender paradigms and the categorization of gendered identities and communities.

The transgender community and scholars who researched transgender identity and processes advanced the argument that gender identity is discrete from sexual orientation. It was important for the transsexual community as an emergent political force to make an argument that distinguished them from the gay and lesbian community that also had its share of "queer" gender identities and performances.

The conflation of sex and gender was identified and argued, reinforced with the voices of the transsexual and later transgendered community. Gender identity was regarded as prior to and distinctive from sexual orientation. Classification schemes that focused on gender status abounded as ethnographers and others tried to make sense of this diversity, including a plethora of gender-bending possibilities, both Euro-American and non-Western. As gendered attributes were juggled and reassembled in complex ways cross-culturally, the problematics of Western categorization in the non-Western context became evident. The tendency for totalizing and grand schemes for classification of gender variance (and indeed I am guilty—Bolin, 1996), has been replaced by a major revolution in anthropology that has led us to reconsider our unitary and inert notions of "third" genders, and even gender itself as far more fluid and contextual than previously imagined (Saunders and Foblets, 2002).

As new generations of anthropologists applied the reflexive and feminist critique, the discipline shifted its focus to the agency of individuals and elaborated themes of individual improvisation, social consensus, and agency. Ethnographies since the 1980s are increasingly dominated by the voices of participants and collaborators. The nuances and distinctions among gendered identities are theorized and contextualized. In this regard, Latin Americanists have contended that sexuality was the primary system for engendering identity; for example, Kulick (1997) engaged a sophisticated argument regarding the *travestis* of Brazil (transgender prostitutes), concluding that although they share a gender with women, they are not women.

Ethnographers with an interest in transgendered phenomenon have made extensive inroads into presenting the voices of transgendered participants (e.g., Nanda, 1999; Donham, 1998, among others too numerous to mention here). However, lest we be too self-congratulatory, a caveat is in order. The reflexive ethnographic tradition, although sharing much with narratives by positioning the voices of collaborators as the cornerstone of the monograph, may inadvertently subvert the very agency they endeavor to demonstrate through the anthropological voice of authority that operates as an etic voice over the emic. In other words, the narrative tradition offers an important addendum to the new ethnography that has already spawned an interesting array of new "poetic" approaches (Ellis, 1997 and Jackson, 1997, among others).

With this in mind, Costa and Matzner approach the last chapter gingerly (Chapter 5, "Analyzing *Sao Braphet Song* Narratives"). In it they identity five themes permeating the *sao braphet song* narratives: (1) identities, (2) definitions and descriptive labels, (3) etiologies of *sao braphet song*–ness, (4) the notion of acceptance, and (5) narrator motivations for participating in this project. These five themes intersect around issues of social identity and the cultural construction of identity, suggesting important insights into the complexity of identity. Each is discussed at length by the authors.

Perhaps, the most salient messages regarding identity are its fluidity, temporality, and partiality (*cf.* Clifford, 1983, 1986). In tandem with a reflexive and feminist stance, Costa and Matzner have confronted prevalent views of the timeless structure of the Thai sex and gender system as either "static and enduring" or ironically "fluid and mutable," but totalizing nevertheless. Their challenge is enacted with the humility that percolates throughout this book; the authors have made no grandiose claims to authority, but rather opted for complicating previous notions that totalize Thai transgender identity as a unitary "third sex" phenomenon. Rather, their goals are to present the heterogeneity of *sao braphet song* through their stories, to emphasize the subjectivity of the narrators, and to request a critical rethinking of extant stereotypes of Thailand's "third gender." Through the words of the *sao braphet song,* the complexity and breadth of identities cross-cuts simplistic and aggregating models of social identity as enduring or fluid third genders. The narrators' stories clearly affirm *sao braphet song* identity at a moment in time, emphasizing the situatedness and contextuality of identities—of "identities in the making" as Costa and Matzner so eloquently suggest. Yet they also argue for the embeddedness of *sao braphet song* identity within the broader Thai ideologies of sex and gender. Thus, the narrative accounts of *sao braphet song* reveal, transgress, and reproduce the Thai sex/gender system, integrating Thai typologies of gender/sex and womanhood as divided between good *"riabroi"* (virtuous) and bad women.

The individual voices of the *sao braphet song* make such complexity visible as some individuals maneuver between *"kathoey"* and *gay,* illustrating the diversity among *sao braphet song,* and others express interest only in "real" men (i.e., gender normative heterosexuals). This close association of *sao braphet song* identity with sexual attraction to males, whether *gay* or straight ("real" men) contrasts with the western transsexual identity, wherein a more protean and fluid sexual orientation may occur for individuals through the life course and at the subcultural level as well (Bolin, 1998, 1988). Costa and Matzner note that the issue of crossing gender borders raises several interesting points of intellectual departure, including the question of the relations between *gay* and *sao braphet song* identities, how the individual's knowledge of identities is situated, and how individuals identify with gender diverse subcultures and the local meanings of those subcultures. That the borders of gendered identities may not be so clearly demarcated is indicated in recent popular and scholarly understandings of "LGBT and Q," wherein "Q" refers to queer or questioning. Recent research on western gender variance suggests that the blurring of identity borders is currently occurring among American teen and young adult lesbian women and FTMs (female-to-male transsexuals) (Weiss, 2007).

THE VALUE OF NARRATIVE AS A HEURISTIC TOOL FOR FUTURE RESEARCH

Male Bodies, Women's Souls is hopefully the beginning of a trend in collaborations between transgendered people in other societies and ethnographers. This is clearly fertile ground for further research as a dearth of literature of personal narratives of transgendered people in cross-cultural settings is available. Specifically apparent is a poverty of *sao braphet song* personal narratives available for public consumption or addressed to scholars. Without the voices of *sao braphet song*, scholars are left with an inaccurate legacy and the public are left to rely on sensationalized media accounts and tourist discourses that perpetuate myths about Thailand's tolerance for the *"kathoey"* "third" gender.

This work offers compelling evidence for the value of the narrative approach for scholars interested in gender identity, gender relations, and the intersections of sexuality and genders. Such an approach offers sharp insights into how individual's motives and identities, that is, their subjectivities, are situated and mutable.

In the tradition of feminism and action anthropology the authors state that one of their goals for using the narrative approach is that it "offers a means of advocacy for and connection with other human beings." Such a stance represents the feminist fusion of the personal and the political in a genre of praxis-oriented research for the new millennium (*cf.* Hall, 1996: 78-79). For those conducting research with the transgendered community, this is a compelling reason for continuing to integrate personal narratives in our ethnographic work, emphasizing narratives more centrally, and/or as distinct monographs in the tradition of Costa and Matzner's *Male Bodies, Women's Souls*.

Scholars with an interest in how gendered identities infiltrate and respond to broader systems of gender relations will find this work an invigorating approach and will welcome the voices of *sao braphet song* who speak so directly to their readers. Although Costa and Matzner have identified five salient themes addressed in the *sao braphet song* narratives, they leave us with many directions for further research. I am piqued by how so many of the *sao braphet song* state that they felt some relief by finding others similar to themselves in the school system. Exploring the subjectivity of young school-age *sao braphet song* would certainly be a fruitful area of research into cross-cultural "coming out" experiences and what this might mean in a cultural context quite different from Western "coming out." Other topics for future research include the question of globalization and the exportation of the Western transsexual identity. After reading these *sao braphet* narratives, one wonders what the narratives of noncollegiate and/or working class *sao braphet song* would look like. In conclusion, Costa and Matzner have written an important work that is a compass for using narratives as the core for a noncolonial anthropology of gender variance that simultaneously celebrates agency and complicates gendered identities.

Anne Bolin, PhD
Professor of Anthropology
Elon University
North Carolina

BIBLIOGRAPHY

Abu-Lughod, Lila. 1991. Writing Against Culture. In R. Fox (ed.), *Recapturing Anthropology: Working in the Present* (pp. 137-162). Santa Fe, NM: School of American Research Press.

Bateson, Mary Catherine. 1990. *Composing a Life: Life as a Work in Progress-the Improvisations of Five Extraordinary Women.* New York: Plume.

Behar, Ruth. 1994. Dare We Say "I"? Bringing the Personal Into Scholarship. *Chronicle of Higher Education.* June 29, pp. B1-B2.

Besnier, N. 1994. Polynesian Gender Liminality Through Time and Space. In G. Herdt (ed.), *Third Sex, Third Gender* (pp. 285-328). New York: Zone.

Bolin, Anne. 1988. *In Search of Eve: Transsexual Rites of Passage.* South Hadley, MA: Bergin and Garvey Publishing, Inc.

Bolin, Anne. 1996. Traversing Gender: Cultural Context and Gender Practices. In S. P. Ramet (ed.), *Gender Reversals and Gender Cultures: Anthropological and Historical Perspectives* (pp. 22-52). New York: Routledge.

Bolin, Anne. 1998. Transcending and Transgendering: Female-to-Male Transsexuals, Dichotomy and Diversity. In D. Denny (ed.), *Current Concepts in Transgender Identity Toward a New Synthesis* (pp. 63-96). New York: Garland Publishing Company

Bolin Anne. 2004. Genderscapes: Panoramas, Paradigms and Possibilities. Presented at the Institute of Ethnology, Academia Sinica, November 27, Taipei, Taiwan.

Bolin, Anne and Jane Granskog (eds.). 2003. *Athletic Intruders: Women, Culture, and Exercise.* Albany, NY: State University of New York Press.

Brightman, Robert. 1995. Forget Culture: Replacement, Transcendence, Reflexification. *Cultural Anthropology* 10(4): 509-546.

Clifford, James. 1983. On Ethnographic Authority. *Representations* 1(Spring): 118-146.

Clifford, James. 1986. Introduction: Partial Truths. In J. Clifford and G. E. Marcus (eds.), *Writing Culture: The Poetics and Politics of Ethnography* (pp. 1-26). Berkeley, CA: University of California Press.

Costa, D. Margaret and Sharon Guthrie (eds.). 1994. *Women and Sport: Interdisciplinary Perspectives.* Champaign, IL: Human Kinetics.

Donham, Donald L. 1998. Freeing South Africa: "The Modernization" of Male-Male Sexuality in Soweto. *Cultural Anthropology* 13(1): 3-21.

Ellis, Carolyn. 1997. Evocative Autoethngoraphy: Writing Emotionally About Our Lives. In W. Tierney and Y. Lincoln (eds.), *Representation and the Text* (pp. 115-139). Albany, NY: State University of New York Press.

Fausto-Sterling, Ann. 2000. The Five Sexes, Revisited. *Sciences* 40(4): 18-23.

Guedon, Marie Francoise. 1994. *Dene* Ways and the Ethnographer's Culture. In D. E. Young, and J.-G. Goulet (eds.), *Being Changed by Cross-Cultural Encoun-*

ters: the Anthropology of Extraordinary Experience (pp. 39-70). Orchard Park, NY: Broadview Press,.

Hall, Ann. 1996. *Feminism and Sporting Bodies: Essays on Theory and Practice.* Champaign, IL: Human Kinetics.

Herdt, G. (ed.). 1994. *Third Sex, Third Gender.* New York: Zone.

Jackson, Michael. 1997. *Paths Toward a Clearing: Radical Empiricism and Ethnographic Inquiry.* Bloomington, IN: Indiana University Press.

Jackson, Peter. 1997. Kathoey><Gay><Man: The Historical Emergence of Gay Male Identity in Thailand. In L. Manderson and M. Jolly (eds.), *Sites of Desire: Economies of Pleasure: Sexualities in Asia and the Pacific* (pp. 166-90). Chicago, IL: University of Chicago Press.

Jacobs, Sue-Ellen. 1994. Native American Two-Spirits. *Anthropology Newsletter* 35(8): 7.

Kessler, S. and W. McKenna. 1978. *Gender: An Ethnomethodological Approach.* New York: John Wiley and Sons.

Kulick, Don. 1997. The Gender of Brazilian Transgendered Prostitutes. *American Anthropologist* 99(3): 574-585.

Martin, M.K. and B. Voorhies. 1975. *Female of the Species.* New York: Columbia University Press.

Mascia-Lees, Frances E. and Nancy J. Black. 2000. *Gender and Anthropology.* Prospect Heights, IL: Waveland Press, Inc.

Matzner, Andrew. 2001. The Complexities of Acceptance: Thai Student Attitudes Toward *Kathoey. Crossroads* 15(2): 71-93.

Money, John and Anke A. Ehrhardt. 1972. *Man and Woman, Boy and Girl.* Balitmore, MD: Johns Hopkins University Press.

Morris, R. 1994. Three Sexes and Four Sexualities: Redressing the Discourses on Gender and Sexuality in Contemporary Thailand. *Positions* 2(1): 15-43.

Nanda, Serena. 1999. *Neither Man nor Woman: The Hijras of India.* Belmont, CA: Wadsworth Publishing Company.

Nanda, Serena. 2000. *Gender Diversity: Crosscultural Variations.* Prospect Heights, IL: Waveland Press.

Saunders, Barbara and Marie-Claire Foblets (eds.). 2002. *Changing Genders in Intercultural Perspectives.* Leuven, Belgium: Leuven University Press.

Skomal, Susan. 1994. Lessons for the Field: Ethics in Fieldwork. *Anthropology Newsletter* 35: 1, 4.

Weiss, Jillian. 2007. The Lesbian Community and FTMs: Détente in the Butch/FTM Borderlands. *The Journal of Lesbian Studies* 11 (3/4): 219-227. Forthcoming.

ABOUT THE AUTHORS

LeeRay M. Costa, PhD, is an Assistant Professor of Anthropology and Women's Studies at Hollins University in Roanoke, Virginia. Her research interests include gender and sexuality, feminist theory, narrative method, nongovernmental organizations (NGOs), women's activism, and movements for social justice. Her work has focused mainly on Thailand where she lived for three and a half years. She is currently working to establish NetworkVA, a Ford Foundation-funded statewide project dedicated to building LGBTQ coalitions across Virginia campuses.

Dr. Costa's work has appeared in the journals *Intersections*, *Transformations*, and *Journal of the Association of Woman for Action and Research*. She also contributed a chapter on Thailand to the *Greenwood Encyclopedia of Women's Issues Worldwide: Asia and Oceania*. Dr. Costa has written for NGO publications as part of her efforts to promote a more activist anthropology and social science. She is a member of the National Women's Studies Association, the Association of American Anthropologists, and the Association for Asian Studies.

Andrew J. Matzner, MSW, MA, is a clinical social worker in private practice in Roanoke, Virginia. He is also an adjunct professor of women's studies at Hollins University. His area of interest is transgenderism in cross-cultural perspective. He is author of the book *'O Au No Keia: Voices from Hawaii's Mahu and Transgender Communities*. He has written peer-reviewed articles on transgenderism in the journals *Crossroads: An Interdisciplinary Journal of Southeast Asian Studies* and *Intersections*. He is also a regular contributor to the *International Encyclopedia of Gay, Lesbian, Bisexual, Transgender and Queer Cultures*, an award-winning online resource. In 2004 he also appeared as an expert commentator regarding transgenderism in Thailand on an episode of the National Geographic channel's documentary series *Taboo*.

Acknowledgments

This book would have been impossible without the eager and sincere participation of *sao braphet song* youth in Chiang Mai. We thank them for the time they contributed to this project, their heartfelt words, and their efforts to create a more accepting, equitable, and just atmosphere for *sao braphet song* and other gender and sexual minorities in Thailand.

We are especially grateful for the unwavering support of our editor, Dr. Eli Coleman. Thank you, Eli, for believing in the importance of this book and for helping to bring it to a wider audience. We also wish to thank our editor at Haworth Press, Tara Davis, for her patience and attention to detail.

Our research in Thailand was facilitated by the Women's Studies Center in the Faculty of Social Science at Chiang Mai University, and the International Sustainable Development Studies Institute. These programs provided office space, access to university resources, and colleagues with whom to discuss our project. In particular we would like to thank Virada Somswasdi and Mark Ritchie. Sasatorn "Doi" Sukharangsan and Aticha Boonprasert played a vital role by typing up the handwritten personal narratives, and we thank them for their assistance. LeeRay's Henry Luce Foundation doctoral fellowship in Southeast Asian Studies at the Australian National University provided an opportunity to begin to translate and think about the *sao braphet song* narratives.

We would like to thank colleagues and friends at Hollins University for moral support throughout the writing process. In particular, LeeRay would like to thank students in her life history/self-narratives class who read and commented on select chapters of this book. LeeRay would also like to thank Geoff White, who both sparked and encouraged her interest in the narrative method.

Andrew would like to thank all of the Thai teachers he has had over the years, especially Ajarn Boonmark, for their patience and encouragement. Finally, Andrew thanks LeeRay for taking him along for the ride.

Male Bodies, Women's Souls
© 2007 by The Haworth Press, Inc. All rights reserved.
doi:10.1300/5750_b

Note on Thai Transcription

We have used a modified version of the Mary Haas transliteration system to transliterate the Thai words in this text. Words have been transliterated so that English-speaking readers will be able to pronounce words as accurately and closely as possible to the original Thai. However, our method does not represent the tonal nature of the Central (standard) Thai language. Following Thai grammar, we do not differentiate between singular and plural nouns, thus *kathoey* is both singular and plural. For place names and some specialized terms (such as *gay, kathoey,* and *sao braphet song*) we have chosen to use commonly accepted transliterations even though these diverge from the transliteration system adopted in this book. Direct quotations follow the transliteration system used in the original text. The names of authors whose narratives are included in this book have been transcribed into English according to their individual preferences.

It is important to note that we transcribe the aspirated consonants *k, t,* and *p* as *kh, th,* and *ph*. These letters are not pronounced as they would be in English. For example, the *kh* in *khon* is similar to the *k* in *king; th* in *kathoey* to the *t* in *tall;* and *ph* in *phii* to the *p* in *pill*. Also, according to Haas convention, the long vowel *ii* (as in *Satrii*) is pronounced as the *ee* is in *tree*. One exception is our transcription of the Thai word *dee,* which is the term's more commonly recognized English spelling.

Following academic practice in Thailand, Thai authors are cited in the text and listed in the reference section alphabetically by their first names. For example, were my (LC) name Thai, it would appear in the references as "LeeRay Costa. 2006," and in the text as "LeeRay, 2006."

MAP OF THAILAND

Chapter 1

Introduction

Diverse genders and sexualities have become an increasingly popular topic among scholars and in popular culture in recent years, yet the experiences and subjectivities of such individuals who may express their genders and/or sexualities differently from the norm remain relatively obscure. In this book we seek to illuminate the experiences of male university students living in northern Thailand who identify as *sao braphet song,* or "a second type of woman," through presentation and analysis of their personal narratives. All of these individuals were born with male bodies, yet they choose to live and/or present themselves to others as women to varying degrees. Some cross-dress, take female hormones, and live as women full-time. Others cross-dress only part of the time or dress androgynously. Some present themselves as men yet claim to have the souls of women.

Sao braphet song are more commonly known in Thailand and the West by the terms *"kathoey"* and "lady boy."[1] In this book we use the term *sao braphet song* because various Thai we spoke with felt that this term was more polite than *kathoey.* Since the term *kathoey* is ambiguous, i.e., it can have positive or negative connotations depending on the context and position of the speaker and can be interpreted as a slur, we decided to use the more neutral *sao braphet song.*[2] Moreover, this was the term preferred by many of the participants in our project. However, we do at times also employ the term *transgender* as in the title of this book. In doing so we use *transgender* in a broad sense to signify a range of nonnormative gender expressions, *not* as a direct translation of the Thai terms *kathoey* or *sao braphet song.*[3]

Sao braphet song are engulfed by stereotypes. When we explored Thai attitudes toward them and stories about them in the mass media we discovered that they are most often characterized by Thai people

Male Bodies, Women's Souls
© 2007 by The Haworth Press, Inc. All rights reserved.
doi:10.1300/5750_01

1

as skilled in the arts of beauty. In fact, many women say that they prefer *sao braphet song* hairdressers and makeup artists. *Sao braphet
song* are also nationally renowned as cabaret performers and are considered by many Thai to be naturally talented singers, dancers, and
costume designers.[4] Yet s*ao braphet song* are also characterized in
negative ways. For example, they are frequently despised for their
tendency to draw attention to themselves through loud and unfemi-
nine voices, revealing clothing, aggressive manners, and "overacting" (see, e.g., Matzner, 2001a).

Western stereotypes about s*ao braphet song* are as superficial as
those found in Thailand: in the mass media they are often featured in
magazine stories about "exotic" Thailand and portrayed as sex workers whose feminine appearance can fool even the most experienced
expatriate sex tourist. In tourist guides Thailand is frequently described as a nonhomophobic and sexually permissive society (Cummings, 1997: 135; Hammer, 1997: 21). *Sao braphet song* are represented as free from discrimination and able to express themselves
without fear of stigmatization or violent reprisals.

Thus, in the popular Thai and Western imaginations, *sao braphet
song* have often served as symbols: of beauty, talent, inappropriate
behavior, prostitution, and sexual freedom. Missing from these representations are the voices and words of *sao braphet song* themselves.
The life experiences of *sao braphet song* are, like any group of people
defined by some shared quality, complex and varied. As the narratives in this book reveal, *sao braphet song* do face discrimination and,
often, physical violence. We believe that a better understanding of
sao braphet song, their subjectivities, and their experiences—as expressed in their own words—will both challenge stereotypes and allow readers to engage with them as individuals rather than as a homogeneous group. Furthermore, these personal narratives will result in
increased knowledge about and insight into the place of *sao braphet
song* in the Thai sex/gender system[5] as well as a more nuanced understanding of Thai sex and gender relations in general.

THE PROJECT

Between 1997 and 1999 we lived in Chiang Mai, the northern capital of Thailand, more than 700 kilometers (about 435 miles) away
from Bangkok. Upon visiting Chiang Mai University (CMU), An-

drew was amazed at the relatively large number of cross-dressing male students on campus. Curious about how such behavior was received in Thai society, Andrew began to conduct research about *sao braphet song* and Thai people's attitudes toward them (Matzner, 2001a). Reports in both tourist guidebooks and Western newspapers and magazines often portray Thailand as a country in which gay and transgendered people are accepted members of society (Anonymous 1996a; Cummings, 1997; Kahn, 1998; East, 2000). Indeed, first impressions suggested that transgendered Thai could openly express themselves in public without fear of harassment.[6] Eager to learn more about the place of *sao braphet song* in Thai society, Andrew turned to the English language scholarly literature. What he found was typically anecdotal and impressionistic rather than information based on in-depth interviewing and/or participant observation (this literature is reviewed in Chapter 2). Therefore, Andrew sought out *sao braphet song* and began to talk to them about their lives. Similarly, he also began to talk to other Thai about their feelings toward *sao braphet song*. As time passed he became less convinced that members of Thai society were as accepting of *sao braphet song* as they had initially appeared to be.

We left Thailand in 1999 and returned in the fall of 2000. Upon our return to Chiang Mai we decided to begin our project on the personal narratives of Thai *sao braphet song*. In the intervening period Andrew had conducted a similar project in Hawaii in which he collaborated with fourteen people living on the island of O'ahu who identified to varying degrees as either *mahu* or transgendered (Matzner, 2001b). He felt the project's narrative methodology was a success because it allowed narrators to tell their stories to a wide range of readers. The participants were enthusiastic about sharing their lives for the purpose of raising awareness and were committed to the project because they had a certain measure of control over the interviewing, transcribing, and editing process. Sharing the book production process with the participants, Andrew attempted to overcome some of the power dynamics inherent in the narrative method and the researcher/subject relationship (these issues are examined further in Chapter 3).

However, instead of a more traditional oral history approach, in the Thai project we opted to take a textual, personal narrative approach. That is, rather than conducting a series of in-depth interviews with each individual, we decided to invite *sao braphet song* to write personal essays about their lives. We made this decision because the oral history interview process is a time and labor intensive one, and because we would have only four months in Thailand to cogenerate the narratives. The sharing of power that Andrew aimed for in his first project and that we felt was necessary in any oral history project typically requires intimate relationships that develop over many months of collaboration and conversation. In addition to the initial steps of establishing rapport and finding time to meet, the process requires conducting a series of interviews with each participant, transcribing and editing interview tapes, and returning transcriptions to participants for them to correct and edit so that they are satisfied with the final product. This process is time-consuming even if only several participants are involved and the interviews are conducted in the interviewer's native language (i.e., English), which ours were not.

Since in Thailand we would be working in the Thai language (in which we are both fluent speakers and readers, but less competent typists) and within a severe time constraint, written essays seemed to be a reasonable and methodologically interesting alternative. By writing about their lives from start to finish with no interruption or guidance by us the researchers, participants would have complete control over how they told their stories. That is, they could faithfully represent themselves to their satisfaction by spending as much time (within a four month time period) as they felt necessary in fashioning and editing a piece of writing.

Although we already knew a number of *sao braphet song* students at Chiang Mai University from our previous stay in Thailand, we decided to post a flyer advertising the project around the CMU campus in order to reach as many potential participants as possible. The flyer (written in Thai) explained that we sought the life stories of *sao braphet song* in order to help people better understand their lives.

Andrew handled the next phase of the project. In meeting with potential participants he explained that we would translate their essays into English and that the finished project would be a book. He asked participants to write about their lives with the aims of educating people and raising awareness about the lives of *sao braphet song*. Andrew also explained that there were no set topics participants were required to address in their essays. However, if pressed he provided some examples such as childhood stories, familial acceptance, societal acceptance, plans for the future, personal feelings in general, etc.

He also requested that essays be between one and ten pages long, and he carefully explained to participants that they need not put their real names on their essays. This anonymity freed individuals to be more honest and open in a society that does not always encourage such personal exposure. To motivate interest and commitment to the project, we offered remuneration for the essays. Certainly this played a role in inspiring at least some individuals to participate.

As the project progressed, individuals contacted us for delivery of their narratives. Andrew typically met participants in a public place where they could present their essays and receive payment. In almost· every case, participants were interested in talking further with Andrew about the project. Not surprisingly, they were also very interested in our motivations as researchers, and we were as open and honest with them as we hoped they would be in return. The participants were often interested in learning more about the situation of transgendered people in the United States. They were often shocked when Andrew spoke about the homophobic and transphobic violence and harassment experienced by gays, lesbians, bisexuals, and transgendered people in the United States.[7] This surprise stemmed from a commonly held belief among Thai *sao braphet song* that attitudes toward sexual and gender expression are extremely liberal in the United States. In fact, many of the participants in our project told Andrew that they looked forward to leaving what they felt was an oppressive social atmosphere in Thailand. Ironically, both Thai and Americans believe the other to be living in a more free and accepting society when it comes to sexual and gender expression.

All of the participants decided to use pseudonyms to identify themselves in the book, and we have made every attempt to protect the identities of the individuals who so willingly shared their stories with us. Andrew also asked for contact addresses so that we could later reach participants if we had any questions about their essays. Andrew began translating the essays into English as he received them. After finishing the translations, we then together carefully edited the narratives without disturbing the internal coherence crafted by the participants. It is important to remember that these individuals are not professional writers. We have chosen not to embellish or dramatically edit their narratives in order to make them more palatable for English readers. Rather, we have endeavored to preserve the flavor of their individual writing styles and the range of emotions that we feel they convey. Hence, we have endeavored to remain as true to the original essays as possible, though translation in and of itself requires interpretation at each and every step of the process.

The problem of translation complicates any assertion that we are simply presenting the "voices" of *sao braphet song* to an English-reading audience, and we discuss this problem further in Chapter 3. As listeners, translators, editors, and researchers, we become the mediators between the actual voices of the contributors and the readers of this book. Hence, it is crucial that we explain what our goals are and situate ourselves in relation to this personal narrative project.

POSITIONING THE RESEARCHERS AND PROJECT GOALS

Throughout the book we identify ourselves as "researchers," "listeners," and "interpreters." Similarly, we refer to those who told us their stories as "participants," "narrators," and "storytellers." We envision participants as active subjects in the narrative process and in their lives in general. Hence, in our analysis we endeavor to avoid language and rhetoric that would make participants into passive objects both of our study and of history. By characterizing the various parties in this way we do not seek to avoid the inevitable power relations that shape our encounter. Our relative education levels, socioeconomic status, temporary residence in Thailand, nationality, and apparent conformity to dominant norms of gender and heterosexuality (i.e., we are legally married) all privileged us (in most ways) relative to the participants in the project. Furthermore, our ability to take their words and make of them what we have here gives us an authorial power with which we are not always entirely comfortable—nor do we feel we should be. It is precisely this tension that keeps us attuned to the power relations that organize our relationships with contributors and that make publication of a book such as this one possible.

But why engage in a project like this? What is the value of the narrative method? What does it have to do with gender and sexuality in Thailand? As stated previously, Andrew initially came to the project with a desire to more deeply understand empirical realities he encountered in Chiang Mai: male university students who openly cross-dress and behave in ways culturally defined as "effeminate." When he found that what he had read in the scholarly literature failed to fully account for the stories he was hearing from *sao braphet song* he decided that further research was in order. Andrew's previous oral history project in Hawaii had demonstrated the effectiveness of personal narratives in addressing problems of gender nonconformity and social marginality. The narrative method not only allowed him and others to hear the voices of those so commonly silenced, but it also provided a venue for narrators to reimagine their lives through their retelling and to create a bridge of shared humanity.

I (LC), on the other hand, came to the project with my own scholarly interests in gender and sexuality as framed through the Thai women's movement and Thai community-based organizations (CBOs) and nongovernmental organizations (NGOs). Although not initially concerned with either "homosexual"[8] or transgendered populations, I quickly found that any real understanding of the Thai sex/gender system would require attention to both of these groups. Indeed, my interviews with Thai women activists revealed attitudes and opinions about same-sex and transgendered behaviors that were as fraught as those about prostitution, one of my primary areas of research (Costa, 2001). Furthermore, I had also utilized the oral life history method in my research with volunteer community activists. I found that it was a productive methodology for accessing individual subjectivity and the ways that gender is experienced in people's everyday lives (see also Personal Narratives Group, 1989).

In conceptualizing this project we believed that by combining our respective areas of research and expertise and by emphasizing the narrative method we could make a significant contribution to our understanding of both *sao braphet song* and the larger sex/gender system in Thailand. Until now no published personal narratives of Thai *sao braphet song* of length have been available in English. In fact, relatively few published personal narratives of transgendered individuals from non-Western countries are available (but see Freeman 1978, 1979).[9] In Thailand, relatively little has been written about or by *sao braphet song,* and this literature is reviewed in Chapter 2. More often than not, scholarly work about *sao braphet song* subsumes them within a larger male "homosexual" subculture (see, e.g., Jackson, 1995a), a rhetorical move that these narratives challenge in interesting ways.[10] Besides the recently published autobiography of a well-known Thai celebrity (Thitsana, 2000), one popular Thai novel about the life of a *sao braphet song* is available, titled *Thang Sai Thii Saam* written by Kiratee Chanar (1993). Suffice it to say that still very little about *sao braphet song* exists in print. Hence, this book is one attempt to fill the existing lacuna and to open up new directions for future study.

It is important to note that we did not conduct long-term, systematic ethnographic research with transgendered youth at the time these narratives were written. Although we do bring to this project a wealth of ethnographic experience (both in Thailand and elsewhere), our experience among *sao brapet song* is limited to observation, casual conversations with friends and acquaintances, and, perhaps most significantly, a limited number of interviews. Unlike other books of personal narratives or life histories (Mintz, 1974; Myerhoff, 1974, 1979; Behar, 1993; Caplan, 1997), the individuals whose stories are presented here cannot be considered close friends or confidants of the researchers. Although this certainly has its drawbacks in terms of a conventional and more traditional ethnographic study, it does not necessarily lessen the importance of the goals of this project. Since three of our main objectives are to (1) stress the utility of the narrative method in general, (2) to provide yet another approach within it (i.e., written personal essays),[11] and (3) to highlight the narrative method's usefulness in studying gender and sexuality in particular, we believe that these narratives provide a unique contribution in and of themselves. If anything they provide a space for the voices of *sao braphet song* to be heard and read.

Indeed these narratives (and this project) offer another set of contributions that are humanistic in scope and purpose. As it has been written, "No more elegant tool exists to describe the human condition than the personal narrative" (Shostak, 1989: 239). The narratives of *sao braphet song* provide for us a window into the lives and experiences of a group of people about whom little is known but much is assumed. In these narratives *sao braphet song* share their joys, losses, accomplishments, goals, hopes and fears, and suffering. They remind us of what it means to be human even as they show us that life can be lived in many ways. *Male Bodies, Women's Souls* is our attempt, together with the participants, to challenge stereotypes, increase knowledge, and build understanding about what it is like to cross socially approved and systematically reinforced gender boundaries in Thailand. It is our effort to listen, and to assist others in doing the same.

WHY "PERSONAL NARRATIVE"?

We have already stated why we believe the narrative method to be so important, and we discuss these reasons further in Chapter 3, but it is important to emphasize that personal narratives provide us with a tale of the self, a story of what it means to be "me." For scholars interested in subjectivity and the creation of meaning especially as it is related to gender and sexuality, personal narratives provide an opportune methodology. For personal narratives, particularly in the case of written personal essays, offer a public construction of self that can be encountered without invasive probing or psychoanalyzing. Narratives can be examined for their construction, their themes, and their exclusions, and we discuss these topics in Chapter 5.

Why select the term *personal narratives*? In talking and writing about the personal narratives of individual people, scholars in various disciplines have employed a range of terms. Some alternative phrasings include life history, life story, autobiography, biography, and self-narrative. Each of these terms is laden with slightly different meanings, both for narrators and for interpreters. For example, the term *life history* suggests that a person's life can be narrated in only one way. Many people take for granted that history is "truth" or "fact." However, in recent decades scholars have drawn attention to the constructed nature of all histories, including life histories (see, e.g., White, 1991, 2000; Peacock and Holland, 1993), thereby challenging conventional notions of "history." Alternatively, the term *life story* suggests that someone's life can be narrated in multiple ways, depending on the time and context of the telling. Scholars such as Brodkey (1987) and Riessman (1993) have chosen to use the term *narrative,* which emphasizes that the story is indeed told by a particular individual. Employing this term aims to draw attention to the vantage point of situatedness and subjectivity from which the story is told, which is inevitably a partial one (Haraway, 1988). *Self-narrative* emphasizes that narratives not only represent a previously occurring series of events as experienced from a particular point of view, but also construct selves linguistically and semiotically. Finally, the term *personal narrative* is similar, except that perhaps less emphasis is placed on the concept of "self" and more room exists for exploring notions of subjectivity that may vary across cultural and historical context.

In this book we primarily use the term *personal narrative*. We have elected to use this term because *narrative* draws attention to the constructed and political nature of people's stories, and *personal* emphasizes notions of subjectivity and situatedness. Since our project is one that seeks to represent the voices and subjectivities of at least some of Thailand's *sao braphet song,* this term seemed most appropriate. However, occasionally we will also use the term *life story* in reference to the stories individual young people tell about their lives and experiences. Furthermore, when summarizing the arguments of other scholars, we may temporarily adopt their respective terminologies.

Similarly, we seek to avoid the "juke box model" of narratives (White, 2000) and thus endeavor not to use the phrase "collect personal narratives." Geoffrey White notes, "anthropologists talk about 'collecting' life histories in the same manner they talk about collecting genealogies or taxonomies" (2000: 183). This verb, "to collect," suggests that people walk around with set life stories or personal narratives in their heads ready to be delivered at the drop of a hat, that these narratives are "stable, coherent referential forms" (White, 2000: 184). In fact, as many theorists have argued, the narration of a personal narrative is always specific to that time and context, to the audience that will encounter it, and to the political and personal conditions that surround the telling. Personal narratives thus reveal a self and identity in flux, ever responsive to the context in which it finds itself. So to refer to what we do with the narrative method as "collecting" entirely misrepresents the project. In the method and study of personal narrative we prefer the terms *coproduce* or *cogenerate*. These terms suggest that both the narrator and interpreter have a comparable role in the resulting narrative. Interpreters and researchers may ask questions, or may merely provide a venue for the telling, as in our project. The use of these terms is not meant to challenge or disavow the agency of the narrator. Rather, it is intended to highlight the complexities of the encounter from which these personal narratives emerged, even as it acknowledges that such encounters vary.

ORGANIZATION OF THE BOOK

Our book chapters have been organized with a specific purpose in mind. Most important, our intention is to share with English-speaking readers the personal narratives of *sao braphet song*. Because we want to emphasize the words and voices of *sao braphet song*—voices that have for too long been silenced or ignored—we present them in their entirety and as the focal point of the book. However, we believe that the additional chapters of the book will help illuminate the meanings and implications of these personal narratives. Chapter 2 provides a brief introduction to what has already been written about the place of nonnormative genders and sexualities in Thai gender and social relations. In doing so it examines how *sao braphet song* have been represented in Thai and Western research and, more briefly, in popular culture. This review highlights gaps in our knowledge about *sao braphet song* and points to the contributions personal narratives can and will make. This chapter is also intended to provide a richer context for reading and analyzing the narratives themselves.

In Chapter 3 we explore some of the most compelling reasons for using the narrative method in social science research and consider some of its benefits for studies of gender and sexuality. We also discuss some of the ways that the narrative method promotes a more humanistic and participatory social science. We examine the problem of translation within anthropology in general, and more specifically in projects utilizing the narrative method. We hope that this chapter, although brief, will provide a sufficient overview for those new to the narrative method.

Chapter 4 presents sixteen personal narratives in their entirety, including two narratives about the Chiang Mai University club for *sao braphet song* called Rosepaper. The narratives in this chapter are preceded by a brief description of the setting, i.e., Chiang Mai and Chiang Mai University. Some preliminary statements about the contributors are also made before turning to the narratives themselves.

In Chapter 5 we look more closely at the personal narratives of *sao braphet song* and examine some of the themes and patterns that cut across them. Our intention in this chapter is to explore how the voices of *sao braphet song* highlight issues of concern to them, to see how they conceive of their own subjectivities, and to identify commonalities and differences in their lives. Furthermore, we hope that our discussion of dominant themes and concerns will help point to future avenues of research. To that end we make some brief recommendations for those interested in pursuing research on Thai people of nonnormative genders and sexualities in diverse cultural contexts.

Since we seek to avoid suggesting that we can somehow encapsulate all there is to know about *sao braphet song* in a final statement, this last chapter is not intended to be taken as some kind of "conclusion."[12] Thus, our goal is to raise questions for further investigation rather than provide authorial pronouncements and summarizing statements. Given both the logistics and theoretical underpinnings of this project, it is highly unlikely that readers will come away from this book without assuming that we are in some sense the "experts." However, it is our hope that readers will complete the book remembering that all people have stories to tell and that their stories are important. Although we believe any move intended to somehow erase our authority is disingenuous and does a disservice to the *sao braphet song* represented here, we do hope that in this book we have conveyed a sense of respect for and collaboration and fellowship with those who so graciously shared their lives with us. This book is for them.

Chapter 2

Gender and Sexuality in Thailand

We believe that a broader knowledge of Thai gender relations is a necessary prerequisite for understanding *sao braphet song* and the stories they tell about their lives. Therefore, this chapter provides an introductory sketch of the Thai sex/gender system through a selective review of the scholarly literature. We begin by describing Thai gender ideologies broadly and move on to a more specific discussion of the place of *sao braphet song* in the Thai sex/gender system.

This chapter includes both historical perspectives and contemporary research on *sao braphet song*. In addition to establishing a richer context in which to situate the personal narratives included in this book, we also aim to highlight gaps in our knowledge about *sao braphet song* and to emphasize the contributions personal narratives can and will make to such knowledge. We hope that this chapter will provide readers with a useful knowledge base from which to understand and critically assess the narratives found in this book.

WHAT IS "THAI"?

So that readers may maintain a complex understanding of "Thailand" and "Thainess" that recognizes both its heterogeneity and constructed nature, we begin with a brief history of the area today known as Thailand and some of its more prominent cultural influences. We believe this discussion will assist readers in taking a more complex approach to the so-called "Thai" sex/gender system.

Located in mainland Southeast Asia, Thailand has an area of approximately 517,000 square kilometers (approximately 199,615 square miles). More than twenty percent of the country's roughly 64 million people live in urban areas. Bangkok, the nation's capital, is

Male Bodies, Women's Souls
© 2007 by The Haworth Press, Inc. All rights reserved.
doi:10.1300/5750_02

the largest city, with nearly ten million inhabitants. Yet far from being an undifferentiated landmass, Thailand is home to vast geographical diversity and can be divided into four distinct regions: the north, with tall, forested mountains and fertile valleys; the arid northeastern plateau (known as *Isan*); the central region, rich in farmland through which the Chao Phraya river flows; and the rainforest-covered southern peninsula, which stretches down to the border of Malaysia.

Reflecting its varied landscape, Thailand is home to numerous ethnic groups. Although national policy asserts one official language (Central Thai), one religion (Buddhism), and one national culture, a wide range of cultural and linguistic variation continues to exist within Thailand's borders. In fact, today's inhabitants of Thailand might be descended from Mon, Khmer, or Chinese ancestors. Ethnic minorities (such as Hmong, Karen, Lahu, Lisu) living in the mountainous regions of Thailand, as well as Muslim Thai and Malays in the south of the country, further complicate the picture of what is generally glossed as "Thai." In addition, factors such as social class, age, gender, and regional location also shape people's conceptions of gender and sexuality.

Thailand's diversity is largely a result of the region's history, which may be characterized by a series of invasions, mass migrations, and trade exchanges. Hence, it is important to recognize that present-day Thailand, although commonly perceived as a unitary, homogeneous entity with a singular past, is largely a social construction meant to bolster the legitimacy of kings and national governments (Thongchai, 1994).

Besides ethnic and cultural differences, regional and class differences also complicate the notion of a singular "Thai" identity. For example, although the majority of the population still lives and works in rural areas, people often think of Thailand in terms of its largest urban area, Bangkok. At the same time, rapid economic progress and the late 1990s economic downturn have led to large-scale migration between cities and rural areas. In addition, the importation of cultural influences from other countries (especially the United States and Japan) is found in music, movies, television programs, fashion, and translated books and magazines. Such influences and transformations impact different socioeconomic classes in various ways and therefore make it increasingly difficult to make broad generalizations about what "Thai people" think, believe, or do. It is with this critical perspective in mind that we hope readers will engage with the material presented in this book.

IDEOLOGIES OF GENDER AND SEXUALITY

Thai gender ideology consists of ideal beliefs and values about gender and sexuality that shape the ways many Thai people understand men and women and their relationships with one another. For example, it is generally believed that fundamental differences exist between males and females. At the same time, it is commonly acknowledged that distinctive "types" of men and women exist. Hence, Thai notions of womanhood are informed by a division between "good" and "bad" women. Ideally, the "proper" woman is a chaste daughter, a faithful wife, or a caring mother. She is expected to follow appropriate modes of speech, dress, and comportment in both her social and sexual lives. Described as *riabroi,* this "virtuous woman" is skilled in household work, has an agreeable demeanor, and is modest in appearance and manner. She is also more mature, dependable, and considerate than her male counterpart. Taught to be hardworking from a young age, this archetypal woman shoulders the responsibilities for taking care of family (including siblings and, eventually, parents) and household (Muecke, 1992; Van Esterik, 1996).

Reflecting a double standard, women's sexuality is typically restricted and stigmatized, whereas men's sexuality is marked by a great deal of freedom. Accordingly, the ideal woman is conservative in her sexual practices, and virginity before marriage is valued. Once married, women are expected to be monogamous and uninterested in sex, except for the purpose of procreation. Young women are often taught that sex is something dirty and that for a woman to show interest in sex is shameful. Indeed, women who engage in premarital sex are considered polluted, stained, or even "broken" *(sia tua)* (Packard-Winkler, 1998; Lyttleton, 2000). Thai women interested in sexual pleasure for its own sake, have multiple casual sexual partners, or engage in sex work are considered "bad." They are considered dangerous, both individually and socially, since their sexual freedom challenges the values of chastity and monogamy and reveals a category of women unconstrained by marriage and/or male control.

Men's sexual desire, on the other hand, is typically valorized and encouraged from a young age. Male sexuality is seen as an instinctive and uncontrollable drive possessed by all men. This sex drive is frequently compared to "hunger," and male sexual appetites must be regularly sated (Van Esterik, 2000: 193). Thus, according to common understandings, men will continually seek to follow through on their sexual "instincts." Men's compelling need for sex—and women's acknowledgement of this aspect of masculinity—is amply illustrated in a 1990 urban Thai survey conducted by the Deemar Company, in which 80 percent of adult Thai men and 75 percent of adult Thai women agreed with the statement that "it is natural for a man to pursue sex at every opportunity" (Deemar, 1990, cited in Knodel, et al., 1999: 96). The idea of an essential, uncontrollable nature of male sexuality is coupled with the belief that men require diversity in their sexual practices and partners, evidenced in the popular phrase that men like to "sample many flavors." The (false) assumption that wives do not have an interest in sex leads husbands to both believe and state that sexual relations within marriage are boring *(beua)*. Such cultural expectations lead to resignation among wives that their husbands will engage in extramarital sex to satisfy their desires. Male sexual outlets include both minor wives *(mia noi),* who function as mistresses, and commercial sex workers (Packard-Winkler, 1998; Lyttleton, 2000).

Interestingly, however, the idea of the hypersexual Thai male, epitomized by the *nakleng* or macho outlaw character, coexists with the other masculine ideal of the celibate Buddhist monk. Historically, Thai males temporarily joined the monkhood before marriage as a rite of passage (Keyes, 1986; Whittaker, 2002). Many men continue to practice this tradition, although it is waning in some areas and young men now enter the monkhood for shorter and shorter periods of time. As monks, men must follow the Buddhist teachings that stress the suppression of the male sex drive. Accordingly, monks are not permitted to engage in actions that might lead them into temptation, such as touching a woman. Although sexual desire is seen as contrary to Buddhist teachings and as an obstacle to enlightenment, a man's appetite for sex and variation of sexual partners is often seen by both men and women to be a "natural" part of what it means to be a Thai man (Keyes, 1984, 1986).

ALTERNATIVE GENDERS AND SEXUALITIES

It is only in recent years that scholars have moved beyond their focus on "heterosexual"[1] identity and desire in the Thai context, as more work has begun to examine marginalized gender and sexual minorities including lesbians, *sao braphet song, gay*[2] men, and male sex workers. Specific terminologies are used in Thailand to refer to varied gender and sexual identities, and it is important to define them here. In Thai, *gay* refers to masculine-identified men who are sexually attracted to other masculine-identified men, and it therefore has a more narrow meaning than its American English counterpart. The term *gay* is distinct from *kathoey,* a word used by some Thai to label feminine-acting and female-identified males. Thus, *kathoey* may be used to refer to those who identify as *gay* but act in an effeminate manner as well as to refer to males who identify as women or *sao braphet song*.

Sexual orientation is tightly bound up with gender identity in Thai discourse in that same-sex attraction is assumed by many Thai people to be intrinsic to cross-gender identity and behavior. *Kathoey* and *sao braphet song* are generally described in both Thai and Western journalistic and academic accounts as men (feminine-identified, but men nonetheless) who are sexually interested in other men. For example, even though the famous Thai kickboxer Nong Tum (who was born male) identifies as a woman (and would be viewed as transsexual or transgendered in Western discourse), she is often labeled as "*gay/ gay*" by both Thai and Western commentators. Such conflation of homoeroticism and cross-gender identity in academic and media discourse and among the general population can cause confusion. For instance, the English word *homosexuality* has been used in the Thai and English print media as a generalized term to refer to alternative genders and sexualities as a whole. This contrasts with Western usage in which same-sex desire can be seen as distinct from transgender identity and/or behavior.

A review of the literature suggests that the majority of research on nonnormative genders and sexualities focuses on male-identified gay men. In fact, the first major work on alternative genders and sexualities in Thailand was Peter Jackson's *Male Homosexuality in Thailand: An Interpretation of Contemporary Thai Sources,* published in 1989. In this groundbreaking text Jackson analyzed letters and responses written by *gay* men and *kathoey* to an advice columnist in the popular Thai magazine *Plaek*. This and other scholarship by Jackson has been primarily text-based and/or has focused on linguistic change among Thai sex/gender categories (see Jackson, 1995b, 1997a, 1999a, 2000). Ethnography on alternative genders and sexualities, in which research is based on long-term observation and interviewing, has predominantly focused on issues of *gay* identity among male sex workers (Storer, 1999b; McCamish, 1999; De Lind van Wijngaarden, 1999). In addition, several large-scale quantitative interviewing projects have investigated incidences of same-sex experience among young Thai men and women as well as the topic of bisexuality (for a summary of these studies, see Jackson, 1999b). Empirical studies have most often been situated within a social services/welfare framework concerned with issues surrounding HIV/AIDS.

Comparatively little in-depth research has been done on the non-normative gender and sexual lives of women, though significant work in this area is now emerging. For example, Megan Sinnott's research, based on extensive ethnographic fieldwork, examines the construction of masculinity among *toms* (masculine-identified women), relationships between *toms* and *dees* (feminine-identified women), and the emergent social and political communities of *toms* and *dees* (Sinnott, 2004, 1999; see also Took Took Thongthiraj, 1994). Ara Wilson's (2004) work, which focuses primarily on the intersection of global economic processes with the production of subjectivities, identities, and intimate relations in Thailand, also provides an ethnographically grounded understanding of *tom* identity and practice.

Less attention has been paid to the experiences and subjectivities of transgendered males. This is surprising given that transgenderism is a highly visible part of contemporary Thai culture. In Thai popular media, stories about *kathoey* are frequently found in newspapers and magazines and appear in television dramas and comedies. In everyday life *kathoey* are quite noticeable as well in urban, suburban, and rural areas. *Kathoey* can be found working in occupations ranging from street peddlers and shop clerks to tour guides and teachers, and are a strong presence in the entertainment, beauty, hair, and makeup industries. Cabaret shows featuring *kathoey* are also popular entertainment venues in most towns and cities.

Despite the pronounced presence of *kathoey* and *sao braphet song* in Thailand, little is known about their lives, struggles, and motivations. Furthermore, the place of transgenderism in Thai history remains dubious. Due to the paucity of both Thai and English written sources, it is difficult to know whether and how transgenderism existed in past times in what is today known as Thailand. Some research clearly demonstrates that transgenderism has long been a part of South Asian and Southeast Asian cultures, and it is reasonable to imagine that those peoples living in the areas today demarcated as Thailand came into contact with such influences.[3] In the remainder of this chapter we discuss transgenderism in a variety of Thai contexts (religious, historical, academic, and popular culture) and examine more closely available information on this marginalized sector of the Thai sex/gender system.

KATHOEY: *SEMANTICS AND IDENTITIES*

Because *kathoey* is the most frequently used term in academic and popular culture discourses to describe transgendered males, we will use this word in the remainder of the chapter. However, we recognize that transgendered males may self-identify using one or more of a variety of terms, including *kathoey, sao braphet song, phuuying* (woman), or *gay*. Hence, it is important to recognize the heterogeneity of the identities to which the term *kathoey* may refer. Our usage of terminology in this section and chapter contrasts with that in the rest of the book in which we endeavor to use the terminology most favored by those individuals of whom we speak. That is, our goal is to utilize terms with which individual subjects feel most comfortable.

Kathoey is a Thai umbrella term that relates both to gender identity and sexual practice. A Thai male who identifies as a man, but who is sexually attracted to other men, may be considered *kathoey*. At the same time, a biological male, regardless of erotic desire, who identifies as a woman may also be considered *kathoey*. Hence, the term *kathoey* as used in everyday conversation refers to both sexual practice and gender expression, thereby conflating what for many individuals are two separate experiences and/or phenomena.

The ambiguity surrounding the usage of the term *kathoey* is clearly evidenced in academic work on alternative genders and sexualities. Although writers describe *kathoey* as "transvestites," "transsexuals," or "drag queens," they typically position *kathoey* within the framework of homosexuality as opposed to transgenderism. For example, some authors have referred to *kathoey* as a type of "male homosexual identity" (Jackson, 1995a, 1997a) or "transgendered homosexual" (Storer, 1999a; Nanda, 2000). Other scholars define *kathoey* as a "third gender," who "may be gay or heterosexual—most often bisexual" (Van Esterik, 2000: 184). Finally, some writers stress the transsexuality of *kathoey*. That is, a *kathoey* is characterized as a "psychological woman born inside a man's body" (Jackson, 1999d: 238). Many *kathoey* consider themselves—and should be considered by others—as women (Beyrer, 1998: 163-164; Brummelhuis, 1999: 127). Still other writers focus on *kathoey* identity in terms of its parodic and performative nature. For example, Rosalind Morris writes that *kathoey* who live as women "live their entire lives in the mode of hyper-femininity. . . Acting kathoey entails the hyperbolic citation of a feminine ideal" (2000: 131).

Some debate exists over the nature of gender and sexual identities in the Thai context. A number of Western researchers have argued that *kathoey* do not necessarily possess a stable identity as such but rather may strategically shift their core identity depending on context. This is due to the apparent plasticity of Thai gender/sexual identities in which males have the ability to slide back and forth along a continuum from "man" to *"gay"* to *"kathoey"* and back again (Morris, 1994b; Jackson, 1997a; Van Esterik, 2000). However, repudiating his earlier work and arguing against this position, Jackson (1999c) maintains that *kathoey* do actually have a stable gender identity, stating that "Thai men who identify as *kathoey,* like many transsexuals and transvestites in the West, often have long histories of cross-dressing and feeling different, of wanting to be women." The notion that a Thai individual's gender identity may not be as fluid as claimed by Western researchers is suggested by the few self-narratives of *kathoey* that have appeared in books and magazine interviews (e.g., Thitsana, 2000; Kiratee, 1993; Wanida, 1999) as well as the personal narratives presented in this book. However, it is important to question whether it is the self-identities that lack fluidity, or the expression of those identities in the form of personal narrative. This point will be discussed further in Chapter 3.

Creation Stories

Thai creation stories provide an interesting perspective on *kathoey* and *sao braphet song* in Thai historiography. Some Western researchers have interpreted the inclusion of a hermaphrodite in Thai creation myths as indicating the "traditional" and long-standing existence and integration of transgenderism within Thai society (Morris, 1994b). One such story is found in the Buddhist palm leaf manuscript collection known as the *Pathamamulamuli*. Translator Anatole-Roger Peltier claims that this particular myth is part of an oral history tradition that dates back to "antiquity" and is distinctly of northern Thai origin (Peltier, 1991: 187). A second, similar, creation myth, known as the Mula Muh, has also been found, but in Mon temple documents. In contrast to Peltier, the translator of the Mula Muh, Emmanuel Guillon believes that this story is "uniquely" Mon and is "part and parcel of their culture" (1991: 22). Although each translator claims that his own version of the myth is indigenous and exclusive to a specific cultural group (i.e., northern Thai as opposed to Mon), both the *Pathamamulamuli* and the Mula Muh relate comparable stories, namely that each of the first two generations of humans consisted of three beings: a male, a female, and a hermaphrodite.[4]

Using Thai mythology to argue for the transhistorical acceptance of *"kathoey"* in Thailand is questionable for a number of reasons. First, no evidence exists that the hermaphroditic figures mentioned either in the *Pathamamulamuli* or the Mula Muh have any connection to those people today referred to as *kathoey* or *sao braphet song* (i.e., biological males who identify as women). Second, it is not insignificant that negative roles are assigned to the hermaphrodites in both the Mon and northern Thai stories. According to each myth, the first generation of humans includes a male, a female, and a hermaphrodite. Yet in both stories, not only is the hermaphrodite shunned by both the male and female, it also commits the world's first murder. Upon discovering that the male and female are in love with each other the hermaphrodite kills the male in a fit of jealousy. The female then buries the male and mourns deeply for him. The myths diverge as they relate what happens in the next generation of humans. In the *Pathamamulamuli* the second generation of beings also consists of a male, a female, and a hermaphrodite. The myth states that after the female and hermaphrodite pass away, the male expresses grief for the female but ignores the hermaphrodite. In the Mon tale the second generation of male, female, and hermaphrodite all exist peacefully without incident. It is curious, however, that in both myths the hermaphrodite disappears from the third generation of humans. Therefore, it is difficult to understand how either myth could be used to show that either a cultural, historical, or even mythological continuity exists with present day transgenderism in Thailand.

Moreoever, it is not clear whether the *Pathamamulamuli* was as popular among the northern Thai as its translator claims. Although Rosalind Morris states that the Pathamamulamuli is "a Lanna creation story that . . . circulates throughout the north in oral stories about the origin of the world" (2000: 127), it appears that this myth is simply one of many creation stories told in northern Thailand. As part of a Tai folklore project, Siraporn Nathalang, a Thai researcher from Chulalongkorn University in Bangkok, analyzed and compared approximately fifty versions of creation myths that she collected from Tai peoples living in northeastern India, Burma, southern China, Laos, northern Vietnam, and north and northeastern Thailand (Siraporn, 1997). Notably, Siraporn's research uncovered no Tai creation myths that include mention of hermaphrodites. Seen in this light, Morris's argument appears to privilege one myth that mentions hermaphrodites over numerous others that do not, thereby raising both methodological and theoretical questions about *kathoey* and about gender and sexual identities in the Thai past.

The specious logic evidenced in Morris's work reverberates in the work of other scholars who have argued that this myth illustrates an unchanging and timeless structure of the Thai sex and gender system (e.g., Nanda, 2000; Van Esterik, 2000; Beyrer, 1998; Herdt, 1997). Taking myths and stories located in particular spatial and temporal contexts, scholars have problematically generalized them to an entire country (itself a recent invention, as discussed previously) that consists of diverse populations. Indeed, it is difficult to argue that any connection exists between the appearance of a hermaphroditic figure in mythology and either the prevalence or supposed acceptance of *"kathoey"* (or *sao braphet song*) in present-day Thailand.

Travelers' Tales

The Thai historical record is largely silent about *kathoey* and *sao braphet song*. Nevertheless, books written by European travelers in the late 1800s offer clues about the existence of transgendered individuals in the Thai past. For example, Carl Bock, a Norwegian explorer who in 1881 journeyed through what is today northern Thailand, mentions in an aside that on his expedition he "heard of several hermaphrodites" (1985: 320). Several years later, in a book titled *A Thousand Miles on an Elephant in the Shan States,* Englishman Holt Hallett recounts an outing he made in 1876 to a city he calls Zimme (the Burmese name for Chiang Mai). He writes,

> Following the road through the western suburb, I entered one of the shops to purchase some Chinese umbrellas, as mine were the worse for wear, and was served by a person dressed in ordinary female costume, who seemed to be very masculine in appearance, and considerably above 4 feet 10 inches in height—a height few Zimme Shan women attain to. On telling Dr M'Gilvary [an American missionary who had lived in Zimme for many years], he informed me that the individual was a hermaphrodite; that this particular form of Nature's freaks was by no means uncommon in the country; and that all such people were obliged to dress in female costume. (2000: 99)

A key source for information about transgenderism in early twentieth century northern Thailand is the Englishman W. A. R. Wood, who first arrived in Bangkok in 1896 as a student interpreter for the British Consul. From the early 1900s until his death in 1970, Wood spent a great deal of time working and living in northern Thailand, particularly in Chiang Mai. His autobiographical work, *Consul in Paradise,* provides an invaluable account of *puumia* (the local term for *kathoey*) in northern Thai society.[5]

> In Siam, especially in the north, there are a certain number of men who habitually wear female clothing and grow their hair long. It does not seem to be thought that there is anything morally wrong about this, and so far as I have been able to make out, these *Pu-Mias* (men-women), as they are called, really possess, as a rule, no moral eccentricities. Physically also, I am

told, there is nothing unusual about them. They prefer to dress as women, and that is all there is to say about it. (Wood, 1991: 98-99)

Wood's comments indicate that public cross-dressing existed in northern Thailand in the early 1900s. Because it is likely that such practices were in existence prior to Wood's observations, we can assume that his observations correlate with Hallet's comments regarding "hermaphrodites" in the latter half of the previous century. Based on the writing of Wood and Hallet, it appears that *puumia* were at the very least tolerated to the extent that they were permitted to cross-dress in public for extended periods of time. Thus, we can find in Lan Na culture a history of transgenderism that extends back to at least the mid to late nineteenth century. Nevertheless, we still have little in-depth information about the place of *puumia* in northern Thai society or knowledge about how *puumia* conceptualized their gender and sexual identities.

RELIGIOUS RITUALS IN NORTHERN THAILAND

Some scholarship indicates that *kathoey* have had—and continue to have—a notable role in the rituals of northern Thai religious life, although in-depth research in this area remains minimal. The religious beliefs of the northern Thai people *(khon meuang)* consist of a mixture of Hindu Brahmanism, Buddhism (Thailand's official faith), and animism—a form of indigenous belief based on the notion that spirits animate all aspects of the natural world, including, for example trees, rivers, and mountains. Spirits play a very important role in the everyday life of many northerners, both rural and urban. One aspect of animism widely written about by researchers is that of local spirit cults. These cults are matrifocal and based on matrilineal descent groups (see e.g., Potter, 1977; Hale, 1979, 1984; Turton, 1972; Wijeye-wardene, 1981). Anthropologist Gehan Wijeyewardene writes, "The domestic cults are basically concerned with women and with women's affairs, with the chastity of women, the purity of the house and domestic tranquility" (1986: 146). Members regularly perform rituals such as the offering of food or incense to various household and ancestor spirits. Cult groups also have mediums, people whose bodies have been chosen by spirits as human hosts. The ritual possession of mediums is a central feature of these spirit cults.

Although spirit mediums are generally women, a small number are males. Wijeyewardene states, "It is often said by Chiang Mai people that male mediums are either transvestites or homosexuals or both—the Thai word *[kathoey]* may be used in both senses" (1986: 159). Morris also notes that the majority of spirit mediums in the cult of Queen Chamathewi, which is popular in Chiang Mai and Lamphun, are *kathoey,* a term she defines as "transvestites/transsexuals" (1994a: 58-59).

Anthropologist Walter Irvine argues that *kathoey* are able to become mediums due to northern Thai beliefs about gender differences. In northern Thai gender ideology men are believed to possess strong souls and are characterized as strongly bounded entities able to easily defend themselves from penetration by outside supernatural agents. On the contrary, women are thought to be weak-souled in that their personal boundaries are less resistant to penetration by external supernatural elements (see also Whittaker, 2000). Accordingly, when spirits (known as *jao*) look for a body to possess they will seek one with a weak-soul that will allow easier access than a hard-souled body (Irvine, 1982: 138). Because *kathoey* are generally believed to be "weak-souled" like women, they too are seen as more susceptible to spirit possession than gender normative men (Irvine, 1982: 225). Irvine suggests that *kathoey* are able to mitigate the social stigma caused by their "gender deviance" by becoming possessed by *jao,* as this "forces" them to become spirit mediums. Having entered into the role of medium, *kathoey* may more freely adopt and perform the feminine role in terms of clothing and behavior, which is necessary for channeling powerful, penetrative *jao*.[6] Notably, as the host of a powerful spirit, a *kathoey* is in the position to earn respect from clients and other mediums (Irvine, 1982: 477). This indicates that *kathoey,* through their involvement in northern Thai religious life, are able to occupy an important, although marginal, space in their communities. It is unclear, however, whether similar ritualistic roles for *kathoey* have existed in other areas of Thailand since research in this area is scant.

KATHOEY *IN THE THAI MASS MEDIA*

Stories about *kathoey* are often featured in the Thai and English-language media in Thailand. Most accounts are superficial and sensationalistic, although a few journalists have written in-depth, sensitive reports that have examined issues such as legal rights, sex reassignment surgery, and social discrimination. Media representations of *kathoey* are important to recognize and analyze because they shape both the assumptions with which and ways that people interact with *kathoey* in everyday life.

Although much media coverage of *kathoey* has focused on their involvement in the entertainment and beauty industries, especially their participation in *kathoey* beauty pagents, a fascination with real and potential crimes involving *kathoey* also appears to exist. One example from the north highlights both the media's attraction to *kathoey* and the ways that Thai social institutions and ideologies construct *kathoey* as "deviant." In December 1996 a *kathoey* in the faculty of education at Chiang Mai University made national headlines for brutally murdering another university student. The publicity surrounding the incident resulted in a public announcement by the Rajabhat Institutes Council, which decides policy for Thailand's forty-one teachers' colleges. The announcement declared that the institutes would begin prohibiting "sexually deviant" students from enrolling in teacher training courses because, in the opinion of council members, transgendered and homosexual teachers were bad influences on young people (Anonymous, 1997b).[7]

The rationale behind the ban lay in Western ideas about human behavior and sexuality and reveals more contemporary mainstream Thai attitudes toward *kathoey* and *sao braphet song*. As Thailand developed and modernized in the 1960s and 1970s, Thai physicians, psychologists, and social scientists were exposed to and consequently adopted a mental-illness model of gender development and sexuality (Jackson, 1997b). This model explains "homosexuality" and transgenderism in terms of pathology, and posits that homosexuality and transgenderism can be caused by environmental factors that occur during childhood, such as the presence of a domineering mother and a passive father. This model emphasizes the importance of boys having strong male role models so that they will develop appropriate gender and sexual identification. For example, a household in which the father is either permanently or frequently absent is seen as negatively impacting a boy's psychosexual development (Jackson, 1997b: 71). Dominant discourses about the origins of "homosexuality" and transgenderism are quite evident in the ways that *sao braphet song* talk about themselves in their narratives, and are explored further in Chapter 5.

The Rajabhat ban led to widespread debate in the Thai media and English-language newspapers published in Thailand. A number of high-ranking Thai government officials, and notably psychologists, supported the Rajabhat ban by arguing that teachers have as much influence on the personality and behavior of children as do parents. Adirek Rattanapanya, chairman of the Association of Secondary School Administrators commented to a journalist that "Teachers are supposed to transfer not only knowledge, but also right behavior" (Anonymous, 1997a). Similarly, Wanchai Chaiyasit, a senior psychologist at the Department of Mental Health stated in a newspaper article that screening by educational institutions for people with "abnormal mental" conditions was necessary to protect students, particularly those under thirteen years of age, from negative influences (Sirikul, 1997). Opponents of the ban consisted of academics and human rights organizations who argued that such discrimination was unconstitutional and violated basic human rights, since every Thai citizen is entitled to equal protection under the law. Although it was never clear exactly how and to what extent the ban was being enforced, by the end of 1997 the Rajabhat Institutes gave in to domestic and international pressure and repealed the ban.

As the Rajabhat debates died down, another media event thrust transgenderism back into the spotlight. In early 1998 Thailand witnessed the spectacular boxing debut of Parinya Charoenphol. Nicknamed Nong Tum, Parinya was a cross-dressing kickboxer from northern Thailand identified in the media as *kathoey*. Initial media coverage of Parinya was extensive, and her story was covered not only by domestic media but also in international newspapers such as *The New York Times* and on television news programs such as CNN. After several well-publicized bouts in Thailand and Japan, Parinya faded from public view, only to reappear as front-page news almost exactly a year later by making public her desire to give up boxing and undergo sex-reassignment surgery. After focusing on a post-surgery career as a club singer, in 2004 Parinya decided to open her own kick-boxing camp (for boys and girls), and in 2006 made a comeback as a (female) boxer.[8]

In March 2000 a Thai film was released that once again put *kathoey* and *sao braphet song* at the center of Thai and international media. *Satree lek* (*The Iron Ladies*) is loosely based on the true story of an upcountry men's division volleyball team whose members were mostly *kathoey*. After winning the national title in 1996, some of the *kathoey* players from Iron Ladies tried out for the national team to compete in international matches, including the 1996 Olympic Games. When none of the *kathoey* players made it past tryouts, two of them complained of anti-*kathoey* discrimination. Indeed, the Thai government believed their presence would cause "friction with less flamboyant team-mates" and would embarrass the country in international matches (Anonymous, 1996a: 36). Chanlit Vongprasert, Secretary General of Thailand's Volleyball Association, stated, "When we travel abroad, foreigners might think Thailand doesn't have enough real men for its team. It would harm our country's reputation" (Smith, 1997). Nevertheless, the film version of the Iron Ladies' saga was immensely popular in Thailand. Directed by Yongyoot Thongkongtoon, it cost under $500,000 to produce and eventually earned almost two million U.S. dollars, making it one of Thailand's highest grossing movies of all time (Horn, 2000). After gaining favorable reviews at international gay and lesbian film festivals, *Satree lek* subsequently opened in general release around the world. On the heels of this film's success a number of other films featuring transgendered characters were produced in Thailand.[9] Hence, Thai social attitudes that define *kathoey* and s*ao braphet song* as "deviant" and "immoral" continue to titillate the masses, ironically keeping them in the public eye.

WESTERN ACADEMIC RESEARCH ON KATHOEY

Little research, ethnographic or otherwise, about *kathoey* and their place in Thai society has been carried out either by Thai or Western researchers.[10] Nevertheless, scholars commonly argue that Thai attitudes toward *kathoey* are generally positive and accepting and that *kathoey* have the freedom to express themselves in public without fear of harassment (Jackson, 1995a: 188; Weinrich and Williams, 1991: 49; Beyrer, 1998; Van Esterik, 2000; Nanda, 2000). Scholars sometimes contrast liberal Thai attitudes with homophobic/transphobic

Western attitudes and—intentionally or not—romanticize the Thai sex/gender system. The Thai sex/gender system is often conceptualized as being more "fluid" than that of the West, which is characterized by "fixed, bounded categories" when it comes to sexuality and gender (Van Esterik, 2000: 213). According to this argument, *kathoey* challenge Western binary thinking and thereby illustrate "the ability of individuals to move in and out of categories" (Van Esterik, 2000: 215: Morris, 1994b: Jackson, 1997a).

Peter Jackson, for example, has made several different assertions about the "acceptance" and "tolerance" of *kathoey*. In an early statement Jackson (1997a) compared *kathoey* and gender normative gay men, arguing that it was *kathoey*'s transgendered behavior that caused them to be relatively more stigmatized. More recently Jackson (1999d) has argued that Thai people are more "tolerant" of *kathoey* than gay men. This is, he claims, because *kathoey*'s outward apperance as women and their "'normal,' heterosexual female desire" locates them within an acceptable framework of gender/sexual relations (Jackson, 1999d: 238). In other words, as long as a couple's gender presentation appears "heterosexual" (i.e., one "man" and one "woman"), then Thai people are more willing and able to understand such an arrangement. *Gay* men, however, violate this framework by being gender-normative men who desire sexual relations with other gender-normative men (Jackson, 1999d: 238-239). Thus, "historically" *kathoey* have "been subject to less intense criticism than open or 'out' *gay* males" (Jackson, 1999d: 230). Jackson acknowledges that although a "presence of discursive sanctions" may exist against *kathoey* among the Thai (e.g., negative stories in newspapers and magazines, scholarly research with an anti-*kathoey* bias), an "absence of practical interventions" also exists (Jackson, 1999d: 241).

However, both Thai and western writers have challenged the conceptualization of Thai attitudes toward *kathoey* as either accepting or tolerant and raise questions about the negative treatment of gender and sexual minorities. For example, in his foreword to a collection of English-language articles on transgenderism and homosexuality in Thailand, Thai journalist Rakkit Rattachumpoth writes,

> Although anti-gay, anti-lesbian and anti-*kathoey* sentiments never provoke any violent homophobic attacks, no Thai homosexual or transgender person feels that they are living in a gay or homosexual paradise. On the contrary, many feel that their lives

are miserable, if not a living hell, where they are threatened
by public denunciation, job discrimination, malicious gossip
and indirect interference in both private and working spaces.
(1999: *xii*)

Similarly, Andrew Matzner's (2001a) research carried out among
university students in northern Thailand also suggests that Thai attitudes toward *kathoey* are ambivalent and often dependent on context.
Moreover, they are intimately shaped by Thai ideologies of sex and
gender. First, it appears that students' feelings about transgenderism
are often influenced by their relationships with *kathoey*. For example,
a person who was loath to have a child who identified as *kathoey*
could simultaneously respect and admire the artistic abilities of
kathoey in general. Second, assumptions about appropriate gender
and sexual behavior also inform students' attitudes. Students indicated that they generally felt positively toward *kathoey* who "behaved
themselves" in public by dressing and acting as modest and appropriate "women." On the other hand, students felt negatively toward
kathoey who drew attention to themselves through loud voices, sexy
clothing, or aggressive behavior—all considered inappropriate for
Thai women as discussed earlier in the chapter.

Some Western researchers have endeavored to explain the reasons
for the existence and apparent prevalence of *kathoey* in Thailand. According to one influential theory, *kathoey* are a necessary component
of the Thai sex/gender system. This is because "A Thai male has traditionally been regarded and has regarded himself as either a 'man' or
a *kathoey*" (Jackson, 1997a: 172). Accordingly, Thai men gain a
sense of manhood by contrasting themselves with *kathoey*: "I am not
a *kathoey*, therefore I am a 'man'" (Jackson, 1995a: 225). In this
model, a *kathoey* is both a "parody" of masculinity, and a "stereotype
of unmasculinity" (Jackson, 1995a: 225). The *kathoey* cannot be
"constructed on the model of a genuine femininity," because "if a
kathoey became indistinguishable from females, his social value in
helping define 'men's' masculinity would cease" (Jackson, 1995a:
225). Anthropologist Robert Levy (1971) has made a similar argument for village Tahitian society. He asserts that transgendered males
(mahu) serve as models of unmasculinity against which Tahitian men
measure themselves.

Such explanations have been challenged for their functionalist orientation and failure to account for the complexities surrounding the

construction of gender and sexual subjectivities. Johnson has criticized Levy's theory because it "cannot account for the varied and multiple discourses attached to and articulated by" those it seeks to address (1997: 23). Similarly, Nico Besnier's critique of Levy's theory argues that "societies offer a wealth of possibilities for distinguishing between women and men, and indeed for creating asymmetries between gender groups" (1994: 306). Although no criticism of Jackson's theory of *kathoey* can be found in print, similar challenges could be posed. Moreover, it is unclear why in the Thai context men would necessarily define themselves and construct their masculinity in opposition to *kathoey* rather than women who are seen as men's opposite and/or complement in many social contexts.

Another theory that attempts to explain increasingly visible numbers of *kathoey* is Han ten Brummelhuis's "global kathoey career" (1999: 123). Based upon eleven interviews with *kathoey,* all of whom were partially engaged in sex work in both Thailand and Amsterdam, Brummelhuis concludes that switching to the female sex offers opportunities to Thai village youths that are not available to them in other ways. In particular, it creates opportunities to leave a poor and boring countryside, to acquire some wealth, and even to migrate to another country (Brummelhuis, 1999: 123).

Brummelhuis's research indicates that gender expression and sexual practice may be manipulated for purely pragmatic purposes, and that an individual's assumption of the *kathoey* "role" may be motivated purely by economic gain. This is similar to reported cases of "heterosexual," gender-normative males who, for monetary purposes, engage in sex work with other gender-normative men. Not insignificantly, it challenges us to think more critically about the disjuncture between behavior and gender and sexual subjectivity, and raises once more the notion of plasticity in the Thai sex/gender system.

At the same time that he implies that any *kathoey* may actually be a heterosexual male in disguise, Brummelhuis argues that *kathoey* "have to be seen as women" (Brummelhuis, 1999: 127). This stems from his claim that the sexual partners of *kathoey* identify as heterosexual, and therefore *kathoey* are rationalized as women, not homosexual men. Although intriguing, Brummelhuis's success in building a persuasive theory about who *kathoey* are as a group and why they do what they do is compromised both by the small number of people he interviewed and the overemphasis on those engaged in commercial sex work.

In conclusion, virtually all of the English-language research has offered sweeping conclusions about the lives of *kathoey* and their place in Thai society. Structural and ideological factors have been emphasized at the expense of gender and sexual subjectivities. How *kathoey* and *sao braphet song* think about themselves *as kathoey* and *sao braphet song* has largely remained a mystery. As we hope our discussion has revealed, a need clearly exists to more systematically seek out and listen to the voices of *kathoey* and *sao braphet song.*

VOICES OF SAO BRAPHET SONG

As we have established, little research on *kathoey* and *sao braphet song* has highlighted *their* voices. Similarly, personal narratives by *kathoey* and *sao braphet song* about their own lives are rare, although some do exist. One early example is *Thang Sai Thii Saam [The Third Path],* by Kiratee Chanar (1993). This is a loosely autobiographical novel about the life of a transgendered youth first printed in serial form in a Thai magazine between 1980 and 1982. Epic in length and scope, this novel provides a beautifully rendered and deeply moving account of identity formation, as the main character seeks to discover and then manifest who she is as a "second type of woman." More recently, Thitsana "Tidtee" Damrongsak (2000), a well-known model, beautician, and restaurateur, who was born male but identifies and lives as a woman published her autobiography.

These personal stories are exceptions, and little interest exists on the part of researchers to listen to or examine the life stories of *kathoey* or *sao braphet song.* Yet these stories are indispensable for a better understanding of how the Thai sex/gender system is constructed and experienced by individuals. In our approach to understanding alternative genders and sexualities, we emphasize personal narratives because they prevent us from simplistically lumping people into categories and instead allow us to focus on the particularities of people's experiences of their sexual and gender identities. In doing so, we seek to challenge theoretical approaches to sex and gender that overgeneralize and fail to take into account how people actively and creatively negotiate rules and norms in their daily lives. Therefore, the personal narratives presented in this project assist us in interrogating broadly defined models of gender and sexuality and in recognizing the particularities that are integral to sex/gender systems. Such an approach allows us to better appreciate the complexity of the Thai sex/gender system, and, hopefully, to work toward a theoretical model that more adequately represents this complexity.

Chapter 3

Narrative Methodologies

As already stated, this book is first and foremost an effort to present the voices of Thai *sao braphet song*—voices that have until now been relatively silenced both at home in Thailand and in scholarly representations circulating in the global intellectual economy. Utilizing the methodology of personal narratives, we have attempted to open up a discursive space in which *sao braphet song* might represent themselves in the form of personal life stories. In this chapter we explain why we favor the narrative method.

WHY USE THE NARRATIVE METHOD?

In the first half of the twentieth century, anthropologist Clyde Kluckhohn (1945) identified both the pros and cons of the narrative method. He cited the scientific problems of "reliability, validity and interpretation" (Mandelbaum, 1973: 178). Because narratives are told by people with imperfect memories, and with an aim toward retrospectively making sense of a life already lived, they are frequently called into question by social scientists with a penchant for positivism and "truth." For example, positivists claim that life history information is difficult to verify, and they assert that both the narrator and researcher are biased. Such criticisms continue to plague the field of narrative studies and highlight the epistemological gaps that exist between different theoretical orientations long ago identified by Clifford Geertz in his assertion that the study of culture is "not an experimental science in search of law but an interpretive one in search of meaning" (1973: 5).

Male Bodies, Women's Souls
© 2007 by The Haworth Press, Inc. All rights reserved.
doi:10.1300/5750_03

Yet Kluckhohn also outlined some of the advantages that the narrative method offers. These include insights into social change and "clues to implicit themes, as documentation on roles, as demonstration of socialization and enculturation, as an entry into understanding personality, as a view of the 'emotional structure' of a way of life, as a means toward understanding variations within a society, and also of seeing the 'common humanity' among peoples" (Mandelbaum, 1973: 178). Many of these advantages continue to be cited today by scholars employing the narrative method. Similarly, Langness and Frank outline a number of positive contributions of the life history method. These include portraying culture or cultural change, illustrating an aspect of culture not typically portrayed by other means (e.g., a woman's point of view), communicating something not usually communicated (e.g., an insider's point of view), answering a question in psychological anthropology (e.g., regarding "deviants"[1]), and, finally, assisting in literary endeavors (1985: 24-29).

But why have *we* elected to utilize the narrative method in our research on Thai *sao braphet song*? Our reasons both overlap with those of Kluckhohn and Langness and Frank, and strike out on new terrain as we seek to utilize the narrative method to answer different research questions and to achieve a more humanistic anthropology in the new millennium. Specifically, we find the narrative method productive for the following reasons: narratives (1) are a universal communicative form and help convey something universal about humankind, (2) provide an entrée into individual subjectivities and into gendered and/or sexual subjectivities in particular, (3) reveal agency and aspects of cultural contestation over norms and beliefs and how certain groups become marginalized, (4) reveal the practices of human transformation, and (5) offer a means of advocacy for and connection with other human beings. Some of these are relatively new reasons for applying the narrative method that reflect theoretical shifts within the social sciences and new areas of inquiry that we are interested in pursuing. Ultimately we choose to employ the narrative method in order to create a more humanistic anthropology that has the potential to assist individuals in recognizing themselves in one another and to create positive social change. In this section, we discuss each of these reasons in turn.

Narratives Are Universal

Historian Hayden White has written that "the impulse to narrate" is "natural" and that narrative is a "panglobal fact of culture" (1981: 1). Similarly, Roland Barthes has noted that narrative is "international, transhistorical, transcultural" (1977: 79 cited in White 1981: 1). Over and over again scholars have emphasized that narrative and storytelling are universal to humankind. Narrative is a fundamental genre of communication (Ochs and Capps, 1996; Riessman, 1993), and hence storytelling appears to be an integral component of our humanity as social beings. Personal narratives convey how we deal with and feel about events, others, and ourselves, but because they are situated in time and space, narratives can only ever be "partial representations and evocations" (Ochs and Capps, 1996: 21). It is precisely this situatedness of personal narratives in which we are interested because it reveals the experiences of individuals whose lives are *not* typical, and more important, not necessarily socially or morally sanctioned.

Everyone enjoys a good story. Moreover, people take pleasure in hearing about the trials and tribulations of others because it allows them to share their joy and pain and to reflect on their own lives in the process. The stories shared by Thai *sao braphet song* in these pages reveal human experience in all its generality as well as its specificity. The narrators express the universal desire to be accepted and loved while at the same time revealing very specific responses and individual choices and indicating a sex/gender order undergoing rapid transition. In summary, the narratives presented here are compelling for numerous reasons, and we firmly believe that readers will find in them both a variety of universal truths about human experience and familiar reflections of themselves.

Narratives Reveal (Gendered) Subjectivities

Personal narratives rely on the voices and experiences of individuals as a starting point from which to understand social and cultural phenomenon rather than simply beginning with the categories and assumptions of the researcher. Narratives are particularly valuable then because they emphasize the lived realities of those people about whom social scientists spend so much time theorizing. One of our goals in this book includes holding in tension both the similarities and differences of *sao braphet song* lives—something that we believe the narratives do very well in juxtaposition with one another and in relation to the experiences of you the reader. We are interested in the commonalities among Thai *sao braphet song,* for these allow us to say something about how such individuals do or do not fit into Thai society, where they are situated in Thailand's sex/gender system, and how those who transgress normative gender boundaries are treated and how they experience that treatment. However, our goal is not to construct some "typical" *sao braphet song* in the service of anthropological theoretical models as was done in the past. As Lila Abu-Lughod did in her work *Writing Women's Worlds,* we present the *sao braphet song* narratives as "a general critique of ethnographic typification" (1993: *xvi*). Indeed, we are also concerned with utilizing these personal narratives as a means of conveying the diversity of *sao braphet song* lives and the situational contingency of the Thai sex/gender system. Finally, we also seek to understand how *sao braphet song* think about themselves as both individual subjects and gendered beings.

Subjectivity might be defined as how one experiences the world as a subject in that world.[2] Subjectivity is composed both of one's agency, that is, one's ability for action and decision making, and the constraints on one's agency, including those larger discourses and structures of power that discipline individuals into conformity with dominant values, beliefs, and practices. In addition, subjectivity includes a person's identity or how one self-consciously defines oneself as a member of some groups and not others. Such identities may be multiple and shifting depending on the context at hand, and may change over the history of an individual's life course. Notions of subjectivity thus overlap with the concept of "self" defined by Ochs and Capps as "an unfolding reflective awareness of being-in-the-world, including a sense of one's past and future" (1996: 21).

Several scholars have emphasized narrative as a way of constructing self or subjectivity (Stewart and Strathern, 2000; Ochs and Capps, 1996). These scholars have examined the narrative techniques used by storytellers to create "coherence" in/of their lives (Linde, 1993) and to project certain kinds of identities to those around them. Although a vast and important literature on anthropological analyses of "self" and ethnopsychology is available (see, e.g., the special issue of *Anthropology and Humanism Quarterly* titled "Notes and Queries on the Broader Implications of the Current Interest in the Study of 'The Self' for the Conduct of Cross-Cultural Research" [1991, Volume 16 (1)]; White and Kirkpatrick [1985]; and Stewart and Strathern [2000:8-18]), we will not explore this literature here. For practical purposes we limit our discussion mainly to the concepts of subjectivity and identity[3] and how these are expressed in *sao braphet song* narratives.

Feminist work on narrative has had the most significant influence on our approach to personal narratives in this project. Feminists have stressed "listening to women's voices, studying women's writings, and learning from women's experiences" as a means of decentering male experience since it cannot possibly typify all human experience (Personal Narratives Group, 1989: 4; see also Shostak, 1981; Abu-Lughod, 1990; Gluck and Patai, 1991; Behar, 1993; Abu-Lughod, 1993).[4] Ever critical of notions of objectivity and the "gaze from nowhere," feminist scholars have emphasized the situatedness and positionality of social actors (Haraway, 1988; Collins, 1990; Harding, 1998). In doing so, they remind us that knowledge and experience are always rooted in a particular social location, marked by relations of power and the intersections of an individual's multiple identities. Hence, positionality must be considered when examining both the encounter of the personal narrative and the narrative produced as a result. Furthermore, relations of power and authority shape the narrative encounter, and researchers should be sensitive to these and how they might influence the narrator's story. We take up some of these issues again in the final portion of this chapter.

Since our interest in *sao braphet song* (as opposed to some other group) derives largely from the way that their lives illuminate issues of gender and sexuality, we are particularly concerned with how their personal narratives reveal gender and sexual identities and the construction of gendered and erotic selves. As feminist scholars have noted, personal narratives "provide a vital entry point for examining the interaction between the individual and society in the construction of gender" (Personal Narratives Group, 1989: 5). For example, Faye Ginsburg's book *Contested Lives* (1989) is an excellent example of how individuals utilize narrative devices to frame their lives and subjectivities. Ginsburg examines pro-choice and pro-life activists in Fargo, North Dakota through the methodology of life stories. She discovers that for both sets of women, abortion activism provides a ground upon which contestation over gender roles and meanings take place. The life stories or personal narratives shared by these activists hence become representations of gender identities and allow Ginsburg entrée into the world of what it means to this group of individuals to be an American woman. Ginsburg writes, "In the ways that the rhetoric and action of abortion activism are incorporated into life stories, one can see how cultural definitions of the female life course, and the social consequences implied, are selected, rejected, reordered, and reproduced in new form" (1989: 62).

Similar to feminist scholars who have turned to the personal narratives of women to understand something about gender relations in the United States, we explore the narratives of *sao braphet song* whose lives, bodies, and practices, by virtue of their transgressive nature, necessitate a consideration of gender and sexual relations, norms, and subjectivities. Some of the questions underlying our research include What does it mean to be a "man" or "woman" in Thai society? What does it mean to behave in a culturally defined "masculine" or "feminine" manner? What happens when one's gender or sexual identity does not conform to that expected by others? and How do *sao braphet song* both challenge and reinforce dominant notions of gender and sexuality in the Thai context? By privileging the voices and personal narratives of Thai transgendered youth, we hope to begin to answer some of these questions and to represent *sao braphet song* such that they will readily recognize themselves and their lives in these pages.

Narratives Reveal Processes of Agency and Cultural Contestation

While the study of personal narratives illuminates individual subjectivities, it simultaneously provides entrée into the prevailing cultural norms and discourses that shape individual subjectivities, thereby elucidating the interplay between structure and agency, or "embedded agency" as Sherry Ortner (1996) phrases it. By viewing narrative producers not as passive objects simply relating a series of "facts," but as creative agents actively constructing identities and negotiating constantly changing realities, we may gain access to processes of cultural contestation, including how individual subjects see themselves as they challenge and resist dominant cultural norms and practices. Personal narratives are thus an especially effective methodology for social scientists because "they illuminate both the logic of individual courses of action and the effects of system-level constraints within which those courses evolve . . . [they] allow us to see lives as simultaneously individual and social creations, and to see individuals as simultaneously the changers and the changed" (Personal Narratives Group, 1989: 6).

The literature on personal narratives provides some instructive examples of how social actors assert agency in contesting hegemonic cultural practices and ideologies. For example, Ruth Behar's *Translated Woman* (1993) relates the life story of Esperanza, a poor Mexican marketing woman. Behar's analysis highlights the ways that Esperanza's personal narrative challenges patriarchal constructions of women in Mexico as well as class inequalities. Through an innovative application of the narrative method, Behar shows us how Esperanza narrates herself not as a passive victim, but as a "transgressive woman," contesting some of the very foundations of her culture. Similarly, Louise Thoonen's (2000) study of female initiation into womanhood in Irian Jaya presents the life history of Maria who, after being initiated according to traditional custom, began to have visions and became a Christian healer and prayer leader. As White states, Maria's story helps to illuminate "the ideological struggle between Christianity and ancestral practices in terms of personal experience and ways of talking about them" (2000: 177). Personal narratives can therefore be crucial arenas of ethnographic information and detail that should not be ignored. Because they reveal struggles over competing identities and how "individuals imagine their own lives in relation to wider fields of identity and power" (White, 2000: 175), personal narratives should be seen as essential to a more critical and humanistic anthropology. In our analysis of *sao braphet song* narratives in Chapter 5 we explore some of the ways that individuals assert their agency and contest a sex/gender system that tends to disparage and alienate them.

Riv-Ellen Prell writes, "Built into life history is the possibility of maintaining the polyphony that we know characterizes human society" (1989: 256). By revealing cultural contestation on an individual level and demonstrating that individual identity, belief, and practice can be expressed in more than one way, personal narratives also reveal the diversity and heterogeneity of cultural (and in the case of Thai *sao braphet song,* gendered) experience. This is particularly important in anthropology, which has for so long trafficked in generalities and typification. If anthropology as a field of knowledge is to truly convey the complexities and contingencies of human experience, then a concerted move away from sweeping generalizations about "culture" and groups of people such as "the Thai" must occur, and more attention must be given to questions of location that ask which Thai, where, and when? As the personal narratives included here demonstrate, gender and sexuality can be experienced and reflected upon in numerous ways, even as a hegemonic sex/gender system continues to reproduce itself. So although we might be tempted to assume that "Thai transgendered youth" all construct and experience their identities in similar ways as a relatively marginalized group, their personal narratives suggest that this is not necessarily the case. It is precisely this diversity of gender and sexual identities that we believe personal narratives can so effectively reveal.

It is not surprising to find then that narrative methodologies have been popular in the study of so-called "marginalized" groups. Groups as diverse as women, homosexuals, poor Guatemalans, and teenage mothers have all been examined utilizing the narrative method (see, respectively, Personal Narratives Group, 1989 and Shostak, 1981; Johnson, 1997; Menchu and Burgos-Debray, 1984; Chasnoff, 1996). Narrative methodologies allow researchers to understand something about groups and individuals who do not conform to mainstream ideology and practice and allow those voices, which so often tend to be silenced, to be heard.

Similarly, it is not uncommon for anthropologists to examine the so-called "margins" as a way of better understanding the "center." For example, Anna Tsing (1993) uses this strategy in her book *In the Realm of the Diamond Queen* as a way to examine fields of power and the ways they are differentially experienced by a variety of located subjects. This approach allows her to understand not only the Meratus Dayaks of South Kalimantan—the "other" to dominant Indonesian politics and culture—but also the dominant groups themselves. As the participants in the Personal Narratives Group have stated,

> Personal narratives of nondominant social groups (women in general, racially or ethnically oppressed people, lower-class people, lesbians) are often particularly effective sources of counterhegemonic insight because they expose the viewpoint embedded in dominant ideology as particularist rather than uni-

versal, and because they reveal the reality of a life that defies or contradicts the rules. (Personal Narratives Group, 1989: 7)

Personal narratives can therefore be viewed as "counter-narratives" that effectively demonstrate that people do not always conform to social or cultural conventions. As we have already discussed in Chapter 2, transgendered people in Thailand have been and continue to be marginalized in a variety of ways.[5] Thus, the personal narratives of *sao braphet song* help to illuminate the shape of the Thai sex/gender system, and at the same time, the ways that the Thai sex/gender system is far less neat, tidy, and orderly than it has often been presented in academic research. It is by relating their personal narratives that *sao braphet song* assert agency, resist dominant gender norms, and most important, transform themselves and their society.

Narratives Reveal Human Transformation

If individual subjects are viewed as active agents in the construction of personal identities, then they must also be understood as having the capacity and desire to transform both themselves and the world around them. Personal narratives thus become a potential and productive avenue for human transformation, as individuals imagine and narrate their lives in a way that challenges hegemonic cultural beliefs and practices. Langness and Frank (1985), discussing the context of the United States, write about "autobiography as transformation" as a way in which the modern individual sees and creates herself or himself. They state that through this medium [of autobiography], people who exist somehow on the margins of mainstream America and its values have shaped self-images of their own design. Among these, blacks, pacifists, women, expatriates, homosexuals, artists, political dissidents, and others have described their own feelings, actions, ideas, desires, relationships, aspirations, and efforts to survive—in their own words (1985: 93).

As "a process of self-creation" (Langness and Frank, 1985: 93; see also Ochs and Capps, 1996), autobiography and the telling/writing of personal narratives allow individuals to imagine themselves anew, in ways not necessarily sanctioned by reigning cultural ideologies and discourses. By beginning with a change in themselves, social actors attempt to change and transform aspects of the society they live in, such as gender ideology, negative attitudes toward nonnormative sexualities, and entrenched relations of power (i.e., class, race, gender, etc.). For example, during the second wave feminist movement in the United States, many women came together in consciousness raising (CR) groups to tell their personal stories. In doing so, they shared their pain, anger, and experience as a way of transforming both themselves and the larger patriarchal social order (Personal Narratives Group, 1989: 261-2).

Narrators frequently anticipate the potentially transformative effect personal narratives may have, and transformation at either or both the individual and social level becomes part of the larger goal in narrating their lives in the first place. For example, Stewart and Strathern tell us about how Ongka (a Papua New Guinea big man who has long been the focus of anthropological research) "wanted a book of his own, to make him famous in the 'white men's world' where the anthropologist's earlier books had been published" (2000: 7). In her book about American abortion activists, Ginsburg (1989) argues that activists' narratives about individual transformations are cast as "conversions," and thus serve as models for imagined social change. Activist women's narratives imagine and construct themselves as certain types of women, and therefore reconstruct gender ideology in particular ways.

The personal narratives of *sao braphet song* may likewise be viewed in such a manner. Similar to abortion activists, *sao braphet song* dispute cultural definitions of gender, both what it means to be a Thai man and a Thai woman. *Sao braphet song*—i.e., male bodies— reject the gender of masculinity and instead claim femininity, its associations, and its meanings. They seek to resolve individual dilemmas that they experience bodily, emotionally, and socially. At the same time many of the *sao braphet song* that participated in this project also stated that they hoped to change the negative ways they are viewed and treated by others. *Sao braphet song* have had to contend with not only the erasure of their individual and diverse life experiences in the scholarly literature (see Chapter 2), but also alienation, ridicule, and emotional and/or physical violence in their daily lives. Through their personal narratives, *sao braphet song* imagine and create selves that address such issues and attempt to resolve some of the dilemmas subjectively experienced. Their personal narratives thus reveal processes of subjectivity formation that are crucial to a more complex rendering of gender and sexual identity. We explore these processes more fully in Chapter 5 when we undertake a closer analysis of the *sao braphet song* narratives presented in Chapter 4.

Narratives Offer Advocacy and a Connection to Others

In their discussion of the narrative method, Langness and Frank ask a crucial question: How can scholars have "a moral effect in the world by making ourselves mediums for the voices of people who should be heard?" (1985: 120). This question emphasizes the narrative method's potential to operate as a form of advocacy and connection to others. Advocacy is apparent in the ways that personal narratives often literally express resistance to a prevailing—and sometimes discriminatory and/or violent—sociocultural order. Narrators advocate for themselves when they tell stories about and critique how their lives have been in the past and reimagine how they might be in the future. Indeed, it is this aspect of the narrative method that makes it so attractive to us as a means of studying the formation of gendered subjectivity. Furthermore, the narrative method, as a form of "tactical humanism" (Abu-Lughod, 1993), makes it possible to both create and reinforce connections between different people, thereby undoing some of the generalizing, othering, and exoticizing tendencies of anthropology.

Scholars engaged in the narrative method may and do become advocates for their subjects, depending on the ways such personal narratives are presented and analyzed. Because of the diverse fields of power in which subjects and analysts are located, advocacy is not necessarily guaranteed. Power relations must be explicitly addressed when utilizing the narrative method and presenting the words of others for a particular purpose. The point is not to speak "for" others; rather, it is for scholars to use their relative positions of power and influence to open up spaces for subjects to speak and write themselves. In her article entitled "Advocacy Oral History," Sherna Berger Gluck (1991) examines these issues in more detail. She uses the narrative method to understand the lives and experiences of both Palestinian and Israeli women resisting the Israeli occupation of Palestine. Taking a feminist—and inherently political—approach to her work, she focuses on using women's voices to advocate on behalf of them and their families. The moral effect hoped for in her book is an increased awareness among Americans (and potentially others in the West) of the occupation of Palestine and an end to the violence it has engendered. Andrew takes a similar approach in his project titled *'O Au No Keia: Voices from Hawai'i's Mahu and Transgender Communities* (2001b). In this collection of personal narratives, Andrew and the project participants share with their audience the experiences of *mahu* and transgendered individuals as a means of creating understanding and acceptance. Many of the narrators speak directly to their readers, advocating on their own behalf.

In our discussion of *sao braphet song* narratives in Chapter 5, we likewise examine how narrators use their written stories to advocate on their own behalf, and we further discuss how our entire narrative project is an attempt to advocate for a people who have been discriminated against because of their expressed gender identity. Our advocacy operates on two levels: representational and material. Not only do we hope to challenge existing representations of *sao braphet song* in the scholarly and popular literatures as discussed in Chapter 2, but we also hope that this book will have material effects on the manner in which *sao braphet song* are treated in their daily lives by family members, co-workers, teachers, religious and community leaders, other Thai citizens, and foreigners.

At the same time, we do realize the limitations of such an advocacy position. First, we were not asked by *sao braphet song* to take on the role of advocate, and perhaps it is imperialistic to think that "we" should be acting as advocates for "them." However, given the negative, overly simplistic, and homogenizing representational treatment of *sao braphet song* (as well as other gender and sexual minorities) in the scholarly and popular literatures, we believe that this is an arena in which we have an obligation to challenge the status quo. By attempting to be as open as possible about our methodological process and theoretical intent, we hope to expose the power relations that structure the narrative encounter as well as the lives and subjectivities of *sao braphet song*. That many of our participants themselves saw this project as a tool for advocating on their own behalf opens up what we perceive as an intersubjective space for us to advocate for *sao braphet song* together.

Second, a palpable tension surrounds any type of scholarly work that is explicitly political and activist in orientation. Although numerous scholars—and especially anthropologists—frequently write in support of the underdog or the relatively powerless, their political positions are not always articulated in any discernable way due to disciplinary pressures. Taking a feminist approach to this issue, we believe that it is crucial for scholars—and especially anthropologists—to be explicitly honest about the partial positions from which they write and analyze. This includes attention to the fields of power in which the anthropologist(s), the anthropological encounter, and its subjects are located. As Abu-Lughod points out, "positionality, feminist theorizing teaches, not only is not a handicap, but must be made explicit and explored" (1993: 6). Moreover, we believe that our work with people who may have been silenced, ignored, discriminated against, or physically harmed requires us to "bear witness" to their plight, as Nancy Scheper-Hughes (1995) has suggested. This may make some scholars who are more positivist in orientation uncomfortable since it challenges the assumed objectivity of social science. However, we believe that this is the only way that anthropology can remain both relevant and humane in the twenty-first century.

Abu-Lughod points out that humanism, although largely critiqued by postmodernist scholars, "continues to be in the West the language of human equality with the greatest moral force" (1993: 28), for it provides one way to connect human beings to one another. She asserts that anthropologists might employ a "tactical humanism" in our work as a means of moving beyond generalizing "ethnographic typifications" and new (postmodern) forms of writing that ironically fail to create the human connection they ultimately seek. In *Writing Women's Worlds*, Abu-Lughod demonstrates this tactical humanism utilizing three strategies that we also attempt to engage with here: (1) making our presence and involvement in the narrative project apparent in the text, (2) focusing on individuals, and (3) using the narrative form (1993: 29-31).

Because personal narratives are rooted in individual experience, reflect the familiar storytelling form, and hence are compelling, they enable the reader's or listener's identification with and connection to narrators. Abu-Lughod writes that "by insistently focusing on individuals and the particularities of their lives, we may be better able to perceive similarities in all our lives" (1993: 27). This emphasis on commonalities is what we so desperately need in today's competitive and highly differentiated world. Through storytelling, narrators and scholars "re-create the human experience" (Langness and Frank, 1985: 136), "[transcend] difference" and "[reaffirm our] common humanity" (Caplan, 1997: 17). By conveying the lives of others, scholars utilizing the narrative method are able to familiarize both their students and the general public with the diversity of lived realities. This aids in breaking down stereotypes and false generalizations and in reducing conflict through knowledge of others in order to help us see ordinary people such as Thai *sao braphet song* as our teachers and heroes (Langness and Frank, 1985: 138-139).

TRANSLATION AND REPRESENTATION

Working with personal narratives cross-culturally raises additional concerns as well. Specifically, in this project we inevitably face the problem of translation: translation from one language (Thai) to another (English), and one culture (Thai) to another (Euro–North American). Translation, or the rendering of a word, phrase, or act in the language and culture of another, is inevitably bound up with *meaning,* one of the core concerns of humans and, thus, of anthropologists. As ethnographers and interpreters, anthropologists are essentially translators. Anthropologists work from the premise that culture is fundamentally translatable, even though they well recognize the potential pitfalls and inevitable relations of power involved.

In a book such as this one, multiple and varied translations come into play: the translation of experience into words by Thai transgendered youth; the translation of Thai words into English words as we, the anthropologists, endeavor to make these experiences/words understandable to an English speaking audience; and, finally, the translation of meaning across cultures. At each step of the process numerous possibilities exist for misinterpretation and error. Walter Benjamin has written that "the task of the translator consists in finding that intended effect [intention] upon the language into which he is translating which produces in it the echo of the original" (1968: 76). He also states that "A real translation is transparent; it does not cover the original, does not block its light, but allows the pure language, as though reinforced by its own medium, to shine upon the original all the more fully" (Benjamin, 1968: 79). Although we aim to express the "intention" and "light" of the original—that is, the personal narratives of Thai *sao braphet song*—we recognize that our translations, linguistic and otherwise, remain representations and not transparent expressions of the original.

Representation has become a distinctly thorny issue in late twentieth and early twenty-first century anthropology. With historical processes of decolonization and national liberation in full swing in many locales, and the emergence of significant civil and indigenous rights movements, the problem of representation has become a hotly contested political issue. Because anthropologists traffic in representations, they have been forced to deal more explicitly and profoundly with the intellectual, social, and political implications of their work. This has resulted in some cases with a turn toward new methodologies, such as personal narrative, and a concern for more explicit reflexivity on the part of researchers. Both of these trends are exemplified in our work, which draws mainly from the work of feminist scholars (i.e., Abu Lughod, 1990; Mascia-Lees, Sharpe, and Cohen, 1989; Personal Narratives Group, 1989; Stacey, 1988; Behar and Gordon, 1995) and anthropologists (i.e., Rosaldo, 1989; Clifford and Marcus, 1986). Yet, by choosing to employ a narrative methodology we by no means suggest that it is a panacea to the continuing intellectual and ethical dilemmas that are part and parcel of the anthropological project. Nevertheless, narrative methodology (similar to visual methodologies such as ethnographic film) forces us to grapple with the issues of representation and power that continue to go unexamined in more conventional ethnographic work. Such issues are particularly relevant in the study of gender and sexual identities since social actors may be marginalized or even become the victims of violence as a result of their gendered and sexual practices.

We acknowledge the difficulties involved in any project of translation/representation, including the possibility for both linguistic and semiotic error. We also recognize that our interpretations of the *sao braphet song* narratives presented in Chapter 5 are partial and situated, and hence posit at best only several possible perspectives. Thus, we encourage readers to seek out their own understandings and translations and to view these multiple interpretations as existing in tension with one another, thereby more fully reflecting the lived realities of Thai *sao braphet song*. We also hope that our interpretations will provoke further discussion and inquiry and contribute to a richer and more complex understanding of gendered and sexual identities, both in Thailand and around the world.

Chapter 4

Sao Braphet Song Narratives

THE SETTING

Chiang Mai is an ancient city that was founded in 1296 by King Mengrai. The people of this region, the Tai, originally migrated from southwestern China into the area presently known as Thailand. In the fourteenth and fifteenth centuries Chiang Mai was incorporated into the Lan Na empire,[2] and became an important cultural and religious center. Eventually the Lan Na empire was absorbed into the kingdom of Siam by the Chakri dynasty. By the turn of the twentieth century Chiang Mai had developed into a bustling center of trade. Social, cultural, and political influences from Burma, Laos, Chinese-Muslim caravans, numerous ethnic hill tribe groups, and Christian missionaries, as well as a vibrant present-day tourist industry, have combined with local cultural traditions and modern technology and industry to turn Chiang Mai into an exciting multicultural city whose population now totals more than 600,000.

Chiang Mai University (CMU), the setting for this project, was established in January 1964, as Thailand's first regional university. The main campus is four kilometers (about 2.5 miles) to the West of the old city of Chiang Mai, and sits at the base of the towering Doi Suthep, a mountain on which rests one of Thailand's most sacred and oft-visited temples. Offering undergraduate, graduate, and various diploma programs, Chiang Mai University has an enrollment of more than twenty-two thousand students. The university is divided into seventeen faculties such as science, social science, humanities, agriculture, education, and engineering, which are further broken down into 107 individual departments.

Although the university must accept a certain quota of students from northern Thailand, and many who attend CMU are either from

Male Bodies, Women's Souls
© 2007 by The Haworth Press, Inc. All rights reserved.
doi:10.1300/5750_04

Chiang Mai or the immediately surrounding provinces, the university still attracts students from every part of the country. Therefore, we include the hometowns of each of the narrators in the headers of their essays along with their academic levels at the time their essays were written.

PERSONAL NARRATIVES

Sixteen personal narratives are included in this chapter.[1] The first twelve narratives were written by *sao braphet song* who at the time the project was conducted were currently attending Chiang Mai University. Each of the narratives is presented in turn. Two of these twelve contributors wrote additional essays about Rosepaper, a campus organization for *sao braphet song* at Chiang Mai University. Although these essays do not focus specifically on the lives of the writers, they do provide insight into a campus organization that has proven to be a great source of support and pride for CMU *sao braphet song*. The Rosepaper narratives provide important contextual information about the lives of its members and reveal the importance of community in establishing and defining one's identity as *sao braphet song*.

One personal narrative was written by a CMU cafeteria worker who is *sao braphet song,* and the final personal narrative was written by a female CMU student who interviewed three of her *sao braphet song* friends. Although these two essays were not written by *sao braphet song* university students themselves, we have decided to include them for several reasons. The cafeteria worker, Mumu, worked in one of the most popular cafeteria stalls on campus and was very open about her gender-crossing behavior. When approached by Andrew to participate in the project she responded enthusiastically. She was only a few years older than the students included here, but she has lived a life quite different from most CMU students. We include her narrative here to highlight both the similarities and differences to be found within the so-called *sao braphet song* community. We believe Mumu's narrative complicates any simplistic conclusions that may be drawn from the other narratives.

The final personal narrative, written by Aom, is yet another innovative approach to the application of the personal narrative method in social science research. This essay is based on Aom's interviews with three of her friends. We liked that Aom came up with an innovative response to our call for participants and that she felt it important to take the time to share with us *her* understanding of her friends' lives. Although this essay falls more squarely within the realm of "biography" than "autobiography" or "self-narrative," it does raise interesting points of discussion about how a self is presented to others and how that self is in turn re-presented by the listener. Unlike the rest of the narratives, this one also represents an appeal by a Thai who is not *sao braphet song* to other Thai to more fully understand and accept these individuals who often face social marginalization and rejection.

Although the narratives presented here have the potential to illustrate many things, we hope that readers will encounter them first and foremost as the personal stories of unique and complex individuals. Although they do at one level convey what it means to be a young transgendered person in Thai society at the turn of the twenty-first century, they are by no means meant to be representative of a "typical" Thai *sao braphet song*, or even of *sao braphet song* attending CMU. Rather, each narrative is an author's attempt to share with others her heart and soul, hopes and dreams. Each narrative offers a unique illumination of its author's thoughts, feelings, and notions of identity, and seeks to assist us, as listeners and interpreters, in better understanding the depth and complexity of the lives of *sao braphet song*.

Dini
Fourth-year student
Hometown: Chiang Mai

I have experienced a great deal of sorrow as well as happiness in my twenty-two years, living the life of a *sao braphet song* or *kathoey* in a country that is rather old fashioned. But there are many *sao braphet song* like me . . .

I was born into a family of four people: my father, mother, younger sister, and myself. It doesn't seem to me that there was anything connected with my family that would have made my heart or behavior deviant. My family is very warm. It is also upper class. My dad is an employee for a private company. He makes more than 40,000 *baht* per month, which is more than enough to allow my mother to stay at home, unlike the case with other families. What I remember most about my childhood is the image of my father and mother arguing. My father liked to drink until he got drunk and passed out. He would come home in such a condition that he couldn't even speak coherently. And he reeked of alcohol. But there was one good thing about my father: even though he got drunk, he never beat my mother.

My mother played a big role at home. It's probably because she was a housewife. So she had the last word in the house. I really admired her, and felt in my heart that she was a hero. At the same time, my father never showed me any love. It's possible I needed love from the same sex. Besides that, all the relatives I grew up with and ran around with and played with were girls. We often chatted about things having to do with beauty, or played with dolls.

My sexual deviance was repressed by those around me until I entered another environment: school. There I met people who had the same feelings and preferences as me. During lunch recess, instead of playing soccer like the other boys (I went to an all-boys school), I'd be with my group of friends who all had the same characteristics, and we'd play games like jump rope or tag. My friends and I would pretend to be female detectives or policewomen. We'd play tag and run around and have a lot of fun, just like girls. Sometimes we'd even scream and shriek like women. When we acted like this it really annoyed our male classmates, but nobody was able to do anything to us. This was because we behaved very well in front of our teachers and always obeyed them. Besides that, our grades were always in the top ten, so our teachers thought very well of us and never disciplined us. But we behaved like this only at school, because when we went back home we had to act like normal boys; if anything, I think we might have appeared a little too well-behaved *(riabroi)*[3] at home.

Actually, I think my parents were afraid that I might turn into a *sao braphet song*. They believed that if I played sports I'd get a strong, tough body and be more masculine. So they sent me to practice swimming, and before long I was good enough to compete. But I guess I wasn't as successful as I should have been; my heart just wasn't in it. Then I had the chance to play tennis and it appeared that I could do it better than swimming because in my first competition I got second place in the ten-year-old division. Therefore, my parents had me concentrate on playing tennis and I was able to do well with it. I competed in Region 5, and once got to the semifinals in the national twelve-year-old division. My parents probably thought that sports would change my attitude, but that wasn't the case at all—the strong motivation getting me to tennis practice every day was that so many of the older tennis players were very handsome! In fact, I became infatuated with an older boy named *Phii* Lok.[4] He was handsome, cute, and very cool. Unfortunately, he had feelings for me only in terms of my being his junior. But then an unexpected situation arose.

When we went away to Phitsanalok province in order to prepare for the Region 5 regional competition, I roomed together with *Phii* Lok. This made me very happy. But I didn't think too much of it until one night when *Phii* Lok came back to the room a little drunk. While I was sleeping I felt there was something touching me. When I opened my eyes I saw *Phii* Lok on top of me. I asked him what he was doing, but he told me to stay still. Then he covered my mouth with his hand. After that he took off his clothes and forced me to take his penis in my mouth. Then he turned and took off my pants and penetrated me from behind. It felt very painful. My tears poured out, but *Phii* Lok didn't care. He continued until he ejaculated inside me. Then he walked off to the bathroom as if nothing had happened! He warned me not to tell anyone what he had done. Because I liked *Phii* Lok I didn't say anything. After that I felt that I loved *Phii* Lok very much, and became very jealous, as if I were his girlfriend. Then I discovered that *Phii* Lok had gotten a real girlfriend and was living with her! I cried and was very sad. I didn't have anything to do with *Phii* Lok anymore.

At any rate, I started to become more interested in beauty arts. I gradually stopped practicing tennis because I was afraid I'd ruin my skin and get muscles. I began taking birth control pills just like my *kathoey* friends at school had recommended so that I could get whiter skin and breasts. Then in the eighth grade the most important event in my life happened: my homeroom teacher invited my parents for a meeting. He reported the matter of my "sexual abnormality" to them, which was the first time my parents had received news about my "abnormality." But when they questioned me about it I denied it. I also promised that I would change my behavior and be a man like I was before. But I didn't stick to my promise—I still took birth control pills and began to dress like a woman in front of other people more and more. Now, as we know, Chiang Mai province is very small; if you do something out of the ordinary the news will quickly spread far and wide. So eventually what I was doing reached the ears of my parents. When I returned home one day something unexpected happened: my parents beat me again and again strongly with a belt, and at the same time begged me to stop behaving like a *kathoey*. I cried but didn't say anything. Finally my parents realized that there wasn't anything that would be able to change me, so they stopped hitting me. My parents gave me a bunch of reasons why I shouldn't be a *kathoey*, to which I listened. An important point they made was that I was the sole male descendent of the family, so it was my responsibility to carry on our family's name. That's why me being a *kathoey* was such a difficult issue for them to accept. But because they realized I would not change, all they could do was warn me, "Don't do anything *'over,'*" that is, in an exaggerated way that would draw attention to myself. They said this because my parents had lots of friends in Chiang Mai who liked to gossip. So I stopped dressing up like a woman in public. But sometimes I went out at night dressed up. I'd take my clothes and get changed at a friend's house so my parents wouldn't find out.

Most people probably think that *kathoey* or *sao braphet song* must have problems and don't have friends. But that's not how it is with me. I have a lot of friends, especially those who are "real men." It's probably because I am a person who is sincere, straightforward, generous, and doesn't act in an overly exaggerated feminine way like other *kathoey* do. This makes my male friends comfortable to walk with me. But when I entered tenth grade—at which point classes became coed—I felt as if the boys suddenly lost interest in me because they shifted all of their attention to their new female classmates. But with the skill in speaking that *sao braphet song* possess, all of us in our small group were able to quickly become close friends with the girls, and sometimes boys would even ask us to help them out by acting as a matchmaker or a go-between to help them meet girls. We didn't complain, and we were always willing to help our classmates.

It was also exciting when I had to start high school military training boot camp. Doing this made me meet many young men from different schools, handsome and not so handsome, nice and not so nice. Whenever we had to do some activity, all of us *sao braphet song* would stick together in a group. Sometimes there was teasing, whistling, and joking from our classmates and the teachers. But it was a good-natured kind of teasing. The instructors didn't try to force us to do things or make us do work that was too rough for us. One could say we were a special case, and this made our fellow trainees envious, seeing that we didn't have to do hard work; we only had to give massages to the instructors and take care of their needs during the training.

At the end of the school term there was a special two-night camping trip. And all the *sao braphet song,* including me, were wanted by the other boot camp students, since being adolescent boys they were horny and wanted to use us to release their sexual tension. There were three boys who wanted me to sleep in their tent, but I refused to go with them. However, they didn't listen and put their hands over my mouth and forcibly carried me to their tent. Two of the boys stood guard outside and the third entered the tent, where he anally penetrated me. Initially I wasn't a very willing participant, but after a while the anal sex stopped hurting as much as it did when they first started. All three boys took turns until each had satisfied his desire. This was a sexual experience I have never since forgotten because it was exciting, painful, and fun all at the same time.

I did the high school military training for three years, and every year we had these camping trips and every year the situation would be the same as before. It reached the point to where we all knew that if a *sao braphet song* wanted to lose her virginity or have a husband then she must wait for the end-of-term camping trip. These relationships were one-night stands; when the sexual activities were over, nobody talked about them.

Soon it was time for me to prepare to take the entrance exam for university. I studied very hard, and did well enough on the test to get into the faculty of economics at Chiang Mai University (CMU). In my new surroundings I had to adjust myself to having more responsibility for my studies. And naturally I noticed all the many young handsome men on campus. I met one man who was in the faculty of engineering. We went to the movies together. We talked on the phone for many months, until his parents found out what was happening and forbade him from ever contacting me again. He had to obey them. This made me very sad and made me think that I didn't want to have any more boyfriends.

When I was on the grounds of CMU I began dressing up more and more. I dressed up as a woman, but not in a skirt. I wore makeup, so sometimes people couldn't tell if I were a real woman or not. In fact, very many men would come and flirt with me. But when they found out that I was *sao braphet song* they'd stop flirting. Because I had been taking female hormones, my body began to change. I looked more like a woman. I had a waist, hips, and breasts. At that point the only thing my parents could do was pray; this was my karma and they couldn't change it.

Then I fell deeply in love with a senior student who was in the same faculty as me. So I searched for his phone number until I finally found it. I called him up and we had a good time talking. Sometimes we'd go out to eat together, and we often talked on the telephone. But it was nothing sexual, nothing more than friends *(phii/nong),* but he did call me "little sister." Then he had to go to America to study, so we were far apart. But we were able to contact each other by e-mail, although not often.

When I was in my second year I wanted to go and learn English in a foreign country. I asked my parents if I could study English for three months during my school vacation. My parents didn't have any objections at all. The study abroad agency that I contacted thought I was a woman, so they put down my name as 'Miss,' which contradicted what was on my passport, so I had a bit of a problem when I went through immigration, but I was finally able to pass through and get on the plane to New Zealand. Nobody on the plane knew that I was a man because I was wearing makeup and had long hair. My body shape also appeared quite feminine.

My host family warned me that if there were any problems I should tell them, because there was homophobia in New Zealand. In fact, they wanted me to keep up my appearance as a woman because they felt it would be safer for me that way, as nobody could tell I was really a man. They also told me that if someone could tell I wasn't really a woman and did something bad to me I should tell them, because in New Zealand individual rights are important and you can sue. My host family never expressed any repulsion or acted differently toward me in any way because of my being *sao braphet song,* but instead welcomed me nicely.

I studied at an English language school, where everyone was friendly and treated me very kindly. I met some Thai people at school, about four or five, who had also come to study there, and we became very close. They all acted as if I were a lady. They honored me in every way, which made me feel very proud. I also met other Thais who had lived in this area for many years. I liked one junior named *Nong* Lek, who was Thai Italian. He had a cute face and was very friendly to me and cared about me more than my other friends. I also showed more interest in *Nong* Lek than in the others. I saw that he had a warm family and learned that his mother, who loved him very much, wanted him to find a good wife and to be successful in life. This meant I felt I had to bring a halt to our deep relationship; we could be nothing more than friends, only *phii* and *nong.* In my heart I felt a terrible pain, but for the sake of the person I loved I was ready to accept that pain in order to give *Nong* Lek a good and successful life. At first he didn't understand why I wasn't acting like before. But finally he understood and didn't put up any resistance. But we still continued to have a good relationship, which has been deep and long lasting. After I went back home to Thailand he came out for a trip the following year. I acted as his guide and showed him all around Chiang Mai. That was one of the best times I've ever had.

While I was in New Zealand for those three months I met boys from different countries. They flirted with me, but since they knew I would be in New Zealand for such a short period of time they didn't devote their full energies to pursuing me—they were afraid they'd be disappointed. So we just stayed friends.

Now it's my last year at Chiang Mai University, my final term. I am planning to go on for my master's degree in another country. I've toned down my feminine appearance, stopped wearing a skirt, and cut my hair. But I can't change my behavior. I don't know if it's wrong or not to have been born like this. But I've never been sad because I feel that I am a human being, just like other people. My parents have often looked down on *sao braphet song,* believing that they are not successful and are deceived by boys who pretend to love them until they are broke, but I firmly believe that I must be a good person and achieve as much success as I can in life in order to prove them wrong. I love my parents very much, and will take care of them the best I can when they get old.

For other people who are *sao braphet song* I send my warm wishes to you and hope that you may successfully overcome your obstacles. I want the people who think that being *kathoey* is all fun and games to know that the life of a *sao braphet song* is not a bed of roses. Every second we face obstacles and difficulties that we must overcome. Only *sao braphet song* who are strong will be able to survive in this world. We must stand on the basis of the truth of being *kathoey.* We must not deceive ourselves, and we must not cause trouble to others. I will surely be single my entire life. Therefore, I must do good so that in my next life I can be born either as a regular woman or man who does not have anything wrong with them, who will have love and not give their parents the sorrow I have given my parents in this life. If you are going to write publicly about *kathoey* in order to let people understand them more deeply, we will support only the story that is the truth; we want to change the attitudes of those who hate us.

Thank you very much.

Lara

Third-year student
Hometown: Chiang Mai

Please call me Lara. I don't know where this feeling I have originally came from. I was born into a family which is almost perfect—it is warm and has a rather good social standing. I can remember that as a child my household contained more women than men. I felt that I was rather close to my aunts. It might have been because I was my parents' first child, and the first grandchild for my grandparents. I received a lot of special attention and care and got a lot of love from everyone. Furthermore, I suppose that the person in our household who had the most power in decision making was my grandmother. I felt that it was really good to be a woman like this.

When I was in grade school my classmates often made fun of me because of the way I was. This made me feel different from them; it made me feel that I couldn't get along with the other students and be a part of their group. So I started to be friends with people who were just like me. I think that if my classmates had not made fun of me at that time, if they hadn't made me out as someone to be laughed at, or as something strange, then I might not have turned out the way I did. Being a *sao braphet song* means you hang out with your own group, not with other students. I was in this group for six years, all during primary school.

After that, when I began junior high school, some groups of my classmates were finally able to accept me, although others still saw me as something to be laughed at. Therefore, the only thing I could think of to make my classmates accept me was to try to study as hard as I could. I made myself stand out in order to diminish my inferiority complex. I was quite successful in doing this. I continued with my diligent study habits because I thought that doing so would give me value and make my classmates want to include me in their activities. I studied hard continuously, and now I am at the university level. I still think that my good grades have been the reason why people accept me. At present my grade point average is 3.47. (I forgot to say that I am in the faculty of economics.) I think that I will continue in school as far as I can go, perhaps even up to a doctoral degree.

Even though at present Thailand has already advanced a lot, one part of society still cannot accept people like me. But I am glad that now society accepts us more than before. Perhaps it is because it is human nature to like to stare at the "defects" of other people rather than look at their goodness. Also, overall, *sao braphet song* appear in the eyes of people as being "abnormal," as men who like men, men who want to be women. Today, there are more *sao braphet song* in society than before, but this doesn't mean that society accepts them a lot more than before (maybe just a little bit more).

Regarding my family's acceptance, I am not brave enough to express my true feelings to them because I am afraid that my parents and others in my family will be disappointed. They will not be able to accept me. So I try not to introduce to them my friends who are *sao braphet song,* or even "real" men and women because I don't want my parents to ask my friends questions about me. I have never brought friends over to my house, and I've never gone to my friends' houses, either. I've closed off every avenue through which my parents might come to know about me. Whenever I do something that is in any way related to this issue, I plan well. I have always had to make my plans in advance in order to prevent news regarding myself from reaching the ears of my parents. That I act like this does not mean that I keep my true self a complete secret all the time, but I will wait for a suitable time to tell my parents—which means I will have to wait for a long time. I must be patient because if I tell my father and mother now, it will surely not be a good thing. I think I will probably have to wait a bit longer to make my parents understand things better than they do now. That is, little by little I will be more open about this issue; it is better to do something like this gradually. The only thing that I think will make my parents proud is my intention to study as well as I can in order to have a good future. This is probably the only thing I can do to make them feel proud of me.

My current challenge is that I want to get first-class honors (3.5 and higher GPA). I need to work just a bit more and then I'll get it; it just depends on my efforts. In the future I'd like to get an MA in another country, possibly America. I think that because of my family's status and my good grades I'll be able to enter a good school—in the top ten—in the United States. I want to finish my MA, and then I'll decide whether to get a PhD or begin working. If I can find a good job in America I might stay there to work. I don't want to come back to face the truth in Thailand, which would be painful and make me unhappy.

I've forgotten to tell you about my hobbies. I like to listen to music, read books, and look at art. My favorite artists are Madonna, Janet Jackson, Mariah Carey, and Whitney Houston. I love their songs, especially those by Madonna. I think she is great, admirable, and very hip! You really could say that almost every *sao braphet song* has Madonna in her heart. We love femininity. We like fashion and performing. We like to follow fashion. We like to design clothes. We like to watch performances, such as concerts, plays, symphonies, etc. Another thing we like is shopping. We often go to department stores to see what is new.

I'd like to try to talk about love. For us, in our perspective, there can be no true love between *sao braphet song* and men. We meet each other in order to leave. So our love is one-sided. We know that he will probably not love us. Even if he loves us, one day he must go back to his previous group, to the way it was before for him; he probably cannot endure the opinions of those around him. Therefore, I try to love myself as much as possible, which is very beneficial for me.

As for changing sex, I've never thought about it. I think that as I am right now people already view me as an oddity, different from other people. If I have a sex-change operation, people will think I am even more strange. Another thing is, because I love myself, I don't want to do something harmful to my body. I am satisfied with who I am. If I did have surgery, I would have it especially for my face in order to improve my looks. For example, something like nose surgery. But nothing else; I wouldn't change any other part of my body.

Finally, I would like those of you reading my story to think over what you have read. Perhaps it will do you some good.

Diamond
Fourth-year student
Hometown: Sukothai

I come from a middle class family that consists of my father, mother, myself, my younger brother, and my mother's mother. My father and mother are both teachers.

I think there are three important reasons why my heart turned to be that of a woman. When I was a child I attended the school at which my mother taught, so whenever there were activities or different performances on stage I was always chosen to participate in them. In doing so I often had to dress up as a woman or wear makeup. Therefore, I didn't have the feeling that there was anything wrong with performing as a woman. In fact, I was actively supported by those around me. The second reason was that I had a closer relationship with my mother than with my father. When I was still a child my father had many friends, and he went out to see them almost every night. He also had a number of mistresses over the years. There were very few times I was able to see my father, so I was actually brought up by my grandmother and mother. The final reason is that my father was an alcoholic, and when he came home for the night he would always look for an excuse to scold or abuse my mother and I. At that time my mother gave birth to my younger brother, and not even a year after that our household had some bad financial problems. This meant that my mother had to work very hard to support our family by selling cosmetics and sweets on the side. I would follow my mother everywhere while she did these part-time jobs. As for my dad, he'd get drunk and then come home and start arguments with my mother and yell at me.

Experiencing this situation made me idolize my mother as a woman who is skillful and is responsible enough to be able to support a large household. I never felt this way about my father. I didn't have any respect or love for my father at all because I thought that in his capacity as the head of the household he should have had more responsibility than he did. Whatever he would do, the rest of us felt it wasn't the right thing. Therefore I began to think that I mustn't be like my father, and instead took up the fighting spirit from my mother. I came up with these three reasons only after I had already entered the university, because being away from home allowed me to think more deeply about the causes of my problems.

As for my behavior as a child, I don't know how other people would have labeled me. But at that time I liked to look at women who were beautifully dressed and imitate them. I enjoyed watching my mother get dressed and put on her makeup. When my mother wasn't home I would try on her clothing and shoes, use a towel as a wig, and put on her cosmetics to make myself up. When my mom found out she would always scold me. I continued this behavior up through the time I entered elementary school. I stopped doing this when I was in the fourth or fifth grade because at that time I was already expressing myself more openly. I had moved to a school in the city center of my province, so I had the chance to make many friends who were "out." Our male classmates made fun of us, calling us "faggot" *(ii-tut)*. But when we were teased, we would say bad things in return.

In the sixth grade I began to feel sexually attracted to a boy who was in my class. When my classmates found out about this they really made fun of me. I cried because I still hadn't truly accepted who I was. My strong feelings about my identity began to first develop when I started high school. Because my school was far from home I had the opportunity to make more friends, and I became very open; I wasn't closeted at all anymore. I already mentioned the first man I had a crush on. But the time I really fell in love was when I was in the tenth grade. It was the love we call "one-sided." I did everything for him. When he got a girlfriend who was a friend of mine who lived close to me I became very sad, and couldn't eat or sleep. I cried for many days. At first, in my heart, I hated that woman. But when I sat down and thought about it, I thought, because I loved him one-sidedly and since he was a "real man," shouldn't he love a woman? Even if he didn't have this girlfriend he still wouldn't be able to love me. It would be better to be friends, because that kind of relationship would last longer. After I reached this conclusion I stopped being sad.

Around this time I began to buy makeup. At school I wore makeup and lipstick, but when I returned home I would clean it off. It wasn't because I had to pretend to be a man when I was at home, but I didn't want to express myself openly around my family because I wanted to respect my parents' feelings. However, I really had to go into the closet in twelfth grade because I got an AFS scholarship to go to Argentina. My host family didn't accept people who are the "third sex" at all so I had to keep my feelings inside. I couldn't express myself to my friends at all. Finally my secret came out, but it was only to a close

Thai friend, nobody else. After that I promised myself that I wouldn't lead a closeted life at all for as long as I lived. Why didn't I accept who I was? I should express my true personality. Keeping this to myself would be unhealthy for my mental state.

When I returned home to Thailand I passed the quota test to get into a well-known university and was able to enter a popular and hard-to-get-into faculty. I was feeling positive and believed that good things would come into my life from then on. My father slowly began to get less strict and my mother seemed to understand me more. When I was at the university the feeling I had of wanting to be a woman grew stronger because I met more friends like me. Plus, I had the freedom to do whatever I wanted—there weren't any people constraining me. So I began to get involved with a group of *sao braphet song*. It's the biggest group at Chiang Mai University, called Rosepaper. I began to take hormones, which we called "hi-tech medicine" *(tek yaa),* and grew my hair out. After I had taken the medicine for a while my breasts began to grow and my face and skin began to look softer and more beautiful. I bought women's clothing and a bra. Finally, I began to perform. We called the *sao braphet song* who perform *"Nang Show,"* that is, "show girls." At first I got the role of backup dancer. My seniors gave me a hard time in the beginning. It was kind of like hazing. I had to carry their costumes, they made me perform without a wig, and they didn't let me make up my face in a beautiful way. When I became a sophomore I had the feeling that I was really a woman, and began to wear the women's uniform to classes. I was also promoted to singer for the Rosepaper performances. I did this until the end of my second year. Then I sat down and thought: Is this all there is to the life that I want? After I graduate, I want to have a different life. I don't want to change my sex. Actually, I don't want to become a woman. Therefore, I completely changed myself to the way I had been before. I cut my hair and stopped taking hormones.

There were two reasons why I made such a drastic change. The first was to give myself a better chance in life, since at present Thai society provides only a small amount of acceptance for *sao braphet song* who are "out." It seems like the only career that is acceptable for *sao braphet song* is that of cabaret performer, which I don't want to do. The second reason concerns my mother. Whenever I went out in public with my mother people would ask her if I were her daughter.

My mother would have to answer that I was her son. I could see that this was difficult for her. Even though she didn't say it out loud, I knew how she felt.

After I had changed myself from being *sao braphet song* there were people who came to talk to me in a way that indicated that they wanted to have sex with me. At first I wasn't picky about my relationships—if a man looked handsome, that was enough. I was like this until my senior year, at which point I began to be very afraid of the modern disease for which there is no cure [i.e., HIV/AIDS]. I was afraid that if I began to have a serious relationship my karma would catch up to me, and I'd have a bad relationship. So I stopped this kind of behavior. Four or five months ago I was in a relationship with someone. I loved this person a lot, but finally we had to break up because he wanted to. I had to spend a lot of time recovering from this. After it happened I got a lot of ideas. For example, I must love myself a lot and be fully aware as I go through life. Loving myself doesn't mean being selfish. That is, we must first consider whether those to whom we give our love are worthy of it. Going through life we must be fully conscious. This consciousness must come from using our wisdom in thinking carefully about good and bad results.

Now I have a relationship with a new partner. We're far away from each other, but we trust each other. This love has been created after careful consideration. I will take care of this love for as long as I can.

Phi

Fourth-year student
Hometown: Chiang Rai

Generally, being a man is something that is a part of a person since birth. But for me, I don't really remember if I have ever felt like I was a man.

My father's work took him to different provinces, and I didn't have the chance to spend time with him. Every day I saw only my mother. I spent all my time with my mother and was close to her—whatever she was doing, I was with her. Whenever I had problems I'd go to my mother and we would talk together like two girls. I did have a younger brother, who was close to my father. You could say that he was my father's child, whereas I was my mother's. But I guess it was good luck that my younger brother wasn't like me because then my parents would have had two daughters!

I remember that as a child I was very close to a female cousin who was a little older than I was. Sometimes I'd sleep over at her house or we'd play house together. Occasionally my cousin would dress me up as a girl. It was a lot of fun, and we spent a lot of time together playing. On the days I didn't see my cousin I'd play with the kids who lived near my house. It happened that there were a lot of girls who lived in my neighborhood, and we'd play shop with each other. Sometimes my cousins and I would play together and dress up in our mother's clothing and have beauty contests. It was a lot of fun.

Both my father and mother spent their days at work, so I had freedom to play as I wanted. I remember once I put on my mother's skirt when she had already left for work. But she unexpectedly came home and found me. My mother was angry and scolded me, but decided not to hit me, so I felt very lucky. I think my father and mother thought that the way I was acting was just something that kids did, so they didn't take it seriously. When I was small I wasn't yet feeling that I wanted to be a woman.

Then I began grade school. I was very well mannered. Sometimes the teachers and my classmates wondered why I was such a polite student. In my first year at school I was made fun of by the other boys. They would mock me by calling me "faggot" *(tut)*. When they did that I would get angry and run after them. Once when I was chasing them I fell and hurt myself. I still have the scar from the cut I got.

When I was this age my father wondered why I wasn't interested in boys' sports, like soccer. Instead, I liked volleyball.[5] My father insisted very firmly and emphatically to my teacher that he should make me play soccer, even though I didn't want to play at all. They forced me to practice, but because I wasn't any good, nothing came of it.

I remember once I saw some girls playing with dolls made out of paper. I wanted dolls like that, but I knew I couldn't ask my mother for money to buy them in case she asked me what I wanted the money for. So I made some paper dolls by myself. However, I had to play with them at school since if I took them home my mother would surely have yelled at me. So I had fun at school; I liked to go to school because that was my chance to be with my friends and play with my paper dolls. But at home I had to act like a "man."

I began to see clear changes in my body in the sixth grade. And it was around then that, for the first time, I began to feel that I wanted to be a woman, and that I was attracted to some of my male classmates. I was also secretly interested in beauty and fashion. But because of my parents I had to keep all of my feelings hidden inside. Then I started junior high school. There was a girl who had a secret crush on me. I found out, but wasn't sure how to act. I had never thought that I'd be in a situation in which I would be involved with a girl. But we started talking, and soon became good friends. However, her friends knew that I wouldn't be her boyfriend. One of them sent me a New Year's postcard, as if she had a crush on me, sending it to me as a way of making fun of me. I didn't know how to react when I got it so I just threw it away. But it made me cry. The students who were around me when this happened were surprised at my reaction. I didn't say anything, but of course the reason why I was so upset was because I knew that I didn't like women. My classmates accepted me for the most part, but I think they thought I was a bit too well mannered. My parents never gave me any problems, probably because I was a good student and had never gotten into any kind of trouble.

At the beginning of my junior year in high school my grades were quite good. I was happy, and so were my parents. I changed schools at this point. When I first started at my new school many girls were attracted to me because I am good-looking. They liked to come up to me and make conversation. I enjoyed talking to them and didn't really think anything of it. This went on until the students started to realize that they had never seen me flirt or have a girlfriend. I remember being asked, "Don't you like women?" I wasn't prepared for this kind of question, and answered that I hadn't thought about dating yet.

In high school all of my friends were women because I felt comfortable hanging out with them. I didn't have any male friends. My father was worried about this and asked me why I didn't have any male friends. My excuse was that the guys at school were doing drugs and smoking cigarettes, and I didn't want to be around people like that. I think my dad saw that by being friends with women I was staying out of trouble. My dad also wondered why I never went out with friends at night. Of course, all my friends were women and they would never go out late at night—they were always at home, so that's where I would be as well. But my father did not give up; he kept badgering me with questions about my behavior.

Toward the end of high school I had a crush on a senior male student. Naturally, I didn't tell anyone about it. I am sure all of my classmates were wondering why I never had a girlfriend, even though I was well mannered and had the looks, which would have made it easy enough. I had to keep all of my feelings inside. I couldn't talk to my parents about it because they were counting on me, as their eldest male child, to be the support for the family. They wouldn't want me to be a *kathoey*. As a result I often felt very disheartened. One problem was that I was really interested in pursuing fashion after I graduated from high school, but when I mentioned this to my mother she responded that she would not allow me go to fashion school because she wanted me to study somewhere closer to home. Therefore, this was a dream that I was forced to suppress. For university I had to choose subjects that my parents approved of, so I decided to study to be a teacher. This was a career that my parents agreed to because, as a government employee, not only would my position be secure, but it would also generate respect from others.

I liked university life because I had more freedom than I had at home. At the university I met new friends who were just like me. Before, I had never gone to class with makeup on, but once in university I began to wear light makeup and to pluck my eyebrows. I wanted to look as good as my friends who were women. I also began changing my eyelashes to look more feminine. When my friends saw what I was doing to my face they asked me about it. I asked them if they thought my face looked pretty. I was feeling more open about who I was. This was probably because I was getting more mature, and because my friends accepted me, and also because society in general was getting more open-minded. But when I went home I had to act like a man. I felt frustrated, but didn't want to upset my mother. I've tried to never give my parents any reason to feel bad. Since I began school I've been determined to get good grades in order to satisfy them. I've never gone out and gotten into trouble or caused them any headaches. I've tried to make up for the fact that I can't be the man my parents want me to be.

As far as love, the love I have known has been different from the love experienced by other people, because my love has always been met with disappointment. I once had a crush on a boy, but he didn't like me back because he was a man—he is supposed to like women. It seems as if this kind of situation is like a rule of nature. But why aren't there any rules regarding love for people like me? Since I love men who are "real" men, it's nearly impossible to be successful in love. But I hope that in the future I will be successful. It has always been painful.

The love of *sao braphet song* is different from that of *gay* people. I have some friends who are *gay,* and it seems to me that love for them consists only of sex, without sincerity. I don't like this because for those of us who want to be women the kind of love we feel is the kind of love a woman feels for a man. That is, a love that must have understanding and caring. Sex is only a part of it. If I love a person I will love him completely. I will always take care of him. But I know he will turn away from me—he will disregard me—when he compares me with a real woman. I have to be the runner-up. I must try to deal with this situation. But because love is something that is natural, I cannot forbid two people from loving each other, or direct someone's love to me. But I still must try, if I am to make myself happy.

Currently I am concentrating on school and graduation because my parents expect that I will become a good teacher, as well as a man, but their expectations are misguided. In Thailand if there is a teacher like me teaching in front of a class, not only will he be ridiculed by his students but he himself will not be satisfied. This is something that makes me realize how things are not the same for some people in Thai society. Sometimes I doubt that equal rights in Thailand really exist for everyone. It doesn't matter if you're a man or a woman, but those rights don't include people like me. Even though society is becoming more open, all too often I've seen the disapproving stares of people when they look at me. Of course, when I see people noticing me, I'd like to think that they were admiring my beauty, but in fact they aren't looking at me in a positive way at all.

At present, the thing I have on my mind is how I can make my parents accept me without causing them pain. If I obey my mother, then I will end up becoming a teacher. But I don't look forward to entering that profession, because in order to be a teacher here in Thailand I would have to be a "man" and keep my true character inside. Yet, if I were a teacher my parents would be happy. Why can't my father and mother accept me? Or have chosen some profession for me that I enjoy? A profession in which I'd be able to express myself, how I really feel? I love designing clothing, just like all the other people like me who make up a large part of the Thai fashion world. I think that clothing and beauty go along with being a woman. But this is difficult for me since my mother has forbidden me to pursue this field. Actually, I just recently spoke to my parents about this issue after having not spoken with them about it for a while. Their position is still the same—they do not want me to study fashion. They also don't want me to let other people know that I am a *kathoey*. I really don't know when my parents are going to learn to accept me as the person I already am.

I am a part of society. This is because Thailand is different from other countries. Acceptance of the "third sex" has really begun to increase. But sometimes it seems as if there isn't any acceptance at all. The working world is one example. There isn't much choice of jobs for a *kathoey*. An important factor is acceptance. Some professions won't allow *kathoey* to work in them, even though in some instances we might be able to do a better job than real men or women. But we don't even have the opportunity to try. If there really were 100 percent acceptance in the matter of work, I would probably end up being a really good teacher. I wouldn't have to pretend to be a man. I wouldn't have to suffer that lie. If there were complete acceptance there would be a lot of options for people like me, and that would make us happy. I am not blaming anybody for how I am. It's just that acceptance would be the best thing for us. It would certainly make me feel comfortable and happy. I deserve this because I've never done anything to hurt another person.

Ping

Third-year student
Hometown: Pattani

A person's life can be compared to the passing of the different seasons, because during your life you will experience many things—both good and bad, sorrow and happiness—all intermingled. It is the same with my own life. In my twenty-one years I have experienced much and had both the best and worst of times. I think this is just the way life is.

I am a native of Pattani province. I was born into a family of civil servants: my father is a government official, my mother a teacher. I have three siblings, all older sisters. I was the last born, the only son. My family is middle class, neither rich nor poor. My family believed itself to be complete because it had a father, mother, and children. But in the midst of that completeness, it seemed to me as if there were some blank space, a gap, within the relationships between these people. In other words, there was no warmth in my family at all. In one week, I would see my father for not more than two days. And every time my father came home, he would argue with my mother. This made me sick of my father's behavior. I thought that my father was the kind of man who is no good, and vowed not to take him as a role model. This is probably one reason that caused me to behave in the way I did (that is, not like other boys), because I admired my mother very much. She was able to be the leader and was diligent in her work; my mother was much more responsible than my father.

I grew up in the midst of a family of women. When I played, it wasn't with guns or tanks. Rather, it was with dolls. Sometimes I played house. Or, if my mother were not at home, I would secretly put on her high-heel shoes and makeup. I would also play "beauty contest" with my sisters. At that time I didn't at all feel that I was different from them, until I entered school. That is when I began to feel different. When it was time for noontime recess, I would sit inside while my male classmates would go and play ball in the field outside. I was very often teased by my classmates as being *"kathoey."* I felt very sad because of this, and sometimes I didn't even want to go to school anymore. But I never told my mother or father about any of this because I knew that they had great hopes for me, as I was their only son.

I endured until I finished elementary school, at which time I was able to continue my studies in the provincial center. There I began to experience a wider, more open society, and met many kinds of people. Junior high was better for me because it was here that I began to express my true self more and more. Being with a group of people like myself gave me self-confidence. I was also accepted more and more by my classmates. This was probably because I did so well in school. I thought that I had to find a strong point to compensate for my weak point. Therefore, I intended to study and constantly keep up my grades.

After I finished junior high school I went to study in another province. My self-confidence was gradually getting stronger and stronger. At this time in my life I had more freedom because I was staying in a dormitory rather than at home. I had freedom in my actions and thinking; I could do what I wanted and experienced all sorts of things. After school I was also working as a food server in a small restaurant. During this time my grades suffered greatly. Finally I began to feel that I had to get serious with my life in my senior year of high school because this was an important turning point in my life: Which direction should I go? I stopped going out and partying. I stopped everything that wasn't good, and set my heart on studying hard enough to be able to get into the economics faculty at Chiang Mai University. I have kept up my study habits right up to today, and as a result of my hard work I have been able to get several academic honors. The thing that constantly pulled at my heart was that I must not disappoint my family. My "sexual deviance" was a thing about which I already felt very guilty.

If one says that love is something that concerns only men and women, then those people who are the "third sex" will certainly contradict this idea, as love can arise in every sex, every person, and in every profession. I have also been in love, a love different from that which parents give their children. It is the love a young couple has for one another. It originally began in high school. I secretly liked one of the senior students at school. I felt great when I saw his face. After this my love gradually developed to the point where he started to show me some love back. If you say that this person was a man, I would have to disagree because he was *gay*. That is, he was a man who also likes men. I loved him very much, and devoted myself to him in every way without ever asking myself whether he felt the same about me. Then we had sex. It was the first time for me, and I began to understand that this person did not love me at all. He only wanted sex. You could say that he had lust rather than love for me. I began to view the love for the same sex as lust rather than love. Thus, I began to hate and fear love. I promised myself that I would never love anyone so completely ever again. But my promise was only words. After I ended the relationship with this boyfriend, I began to feel that I wouldn't be able to remain alone. I felt lonely and started to look for a person to love, even though in my heart I still very much had a fear of love. But this time I handled things by convincing myself that the love between two men is certainly not permanent.

My new boyfriend was a student just like me, but went to a different school. The first time I met him I felt that this person must definitely be the one for me. The two of us hung out like friends who knew each other very well rather than as if we were a romantically involved couple. This was because I thought that our getting together as friends would enable us to have a longer relationship than if we had first gotten together as a couple. We are still together today. We sympathize with each other and always help each other. It is a good feeling that we give to one another.

In Thailand today the third sex is gaining more acceptance because society has become more open and has given the opportunity to them to show their ability, something that society in the past did not do. There are opportunities in many professions. But societal acceptance also has a negative aspect. That is, there are people who oppose the third sex. And some people are quite hateful. In fact, I once had an experience with this kind of person. I had gone to apply for work at a restaurant with my friend. The store's owner stared at me from head to foot. He looked at me with contempt, and refused to consider me for the job. I felt very bad, but was lucky to have had a friend who understood me. I didn't have anybody else. This began to give me encouragement. And my self-confidence, which I had lost, returned like before. I wouldn't just accept the words of those who looked down on me. If we accept those words they will destroy us from the inside.

There is no one in this world who chooses to be born. If people could choose to be born, surely society would be thrown into confusion. Each person would compete with one another to be born into a warm, rich, healthy family. It is the same with the third sex. If they could choose to be born, they surely would choose to be born as a "real" man or "real" woman so nobody would look down on them.

Stop! Stop looking down on and despising the third sex! The third sex are born as human beings, just like other people. They have the same status and freedom of being human just as others do. Give a chance to the third sex.

Marco
Third-year student
Hometown: Payao

A Lavender Life

"*Kathoey*" is a word I have been familiar with since I was a child. It was the term that people used to refer to me. It is surprising that from the first time I heard this word I immediately understood what it meant. It became a word familiar to my ears. I still cannot completely say what the difference is between *gay* and *kathoey* because there is no word for *kathoey* in English. Therefore, if foreigners in Thailand see people who are effeminate, I don't really know what they will call them. But let's understand that it is a group of people who like the same sex.

I have been a *kathoey* since I was a child. My family has four people: my father, mother, younger sister, and me. At the beginning of my life, three months after I was born, my mother took me to be raised by my father's mother because at that time my parents' financial situation was not very good. This was because my parents had me when they were only nineteen years old. My grandmother's house had many people living in it since she had nine children—eight boys and one girl. I was her first grandchild, so I was treated with great affection, like a girl, ever since I was small. Perhaps this was because there were already so many men living in this household. I was quite special for my grandfather, who loved me very much. He wouldn't allow anyone to tease me at all. I lived in this household until I was fourteen and had already graduated from ninth grade. At that time I moved back in with my parents, who were living in another province. Then I had to stay with my maternal grandmother because my parents' work took them to different provinces. I would see them only every two or three months. I lived this way for three more years, after which I came to the university at which I am studying now. I'm twenty years old. Many different things have happened throughout my life that I would like to share with people.

When I was a youngster in kindergarten, I was treated like a girl by my grandmother. The children who lived around our house were mostly girls. I played with them so much that people teased me that I was "*kathoey.*" This made me angry. Why did they have to make fun of me? Not only my relatives teased me, but also friends and neighbors—they all agreed that I was a *kathoey*. I couldn't do anything except be quiet and let them laugh in front of my face. But actually deep in my heart I liked handsome boys. I liked to be with boys who had warm personalities. When there were important festivals the schoolchildren would have to put on a performance. I would often be chosen to be a performer because my aunt was a teacher at my school. There was one play in which there was a shortage of performers. All the roles were for female characters. Since there weren't enough performers I had to be a replacement, which meant I had to get dressed up as a woman. This made the people laugh and there was a good response by the audience. At that time I was very shy, but actually I was happy that I got the chance to dress as a woman.

Later, my grandfather died, so I had to decrease acting feminine because my uncles put pressure on me. They liked to force me to be masculine and make me play in dangerous situations. However, they still saw me as being soft, so once they took me and left me in a cemetery that was diagonally across the street from our house. I was very scared and wasn't brave enough to walk out of it by myself. I just sat there trembling until my grandmother came to get me out. This treatment made me begin to appear more as a man on the outside. My female friends with whom I had played started to turn away from me and stop being friendly. I had to go and find friends who were boys the same age as me in order to cover up that I wasn't a "real" man. However, there was still teasing by my friends. Although it was just play-teasing, it always felt like a knife that pierced me painfully. In running or playing sports, when I lost or made a mistake, I would be condemned with the word *"kathoey."* However, it was good in one sense, in that I began to be accepted by my friends as a regular guy.

I remember in the fourth grade I liked a girl who was in the same class as me. I thought she was cute. We could talk to each other about anything. The feelings I was having made me think that I was fully a man. But in the end it wasn't anything serious, just a crush, because I still had my old preferences.

The subjects at school that I didn't like were physical education and the Tiger Scout program. This was because I was always the lowest ranked, no matter how well I performed. It was as if I had an inferiority complex with these subjects. Even the teachers teased me that it was okay if I didn't do the activities before I had even started them!

Therefore my grade school life had ups and downs; I was confused, like a child. In high school I still had a strange feeling of the sort that I couldn't tell anyone about. But I began to have more friends who were boys. It was as if everyone had completely forgotten my past. It looked like everything in my life was going to be okay. I was living normally and happily in society. I had friends, I had a girlfriend (whom I didn't really love), and I was even actually thinking that I wanted a nice, warm family.

Then in the tenth grade I had to change schools. It was at my new school that I found myself. I chose to study art and French, which weren't at all appropriate for boys, but I studied them because they were my favorite subjects and I didn't care what anyone said. Now that I had moved schools, there wasn't anyone who knew about my past. In my classroom there were forty-one girls and eight boys. At first I acted just like before—as a boy. I thought that this was good, but after mixing more and more with the girls I noticed good things about being a woman and began to change what was masculine about myself. My behavior and manners started to be like those of a woman, so much so that one day a friend came to me and asked whether or not I was a *kathoey*. I thought about this for many days, until I was brave enough to decide that I would accept who I was— and that I really was a *kathoey*. After that, it was something that the teachers knew, and many classmates knew as well about me. I was very happy, just like a bird that has been released from its cage. I began to see my capabilities: I could work rather well with things related to beauty, to the extent that the teachers moved me to the top level in subjects related to beauty and art. I didn't have to keep my feelings inside anymore. I could say and do what I wanted.

Then I began to fall in love with a friend who was a boy. He was very ordinary looking. In the end I had to be disappointed because he was a boy. I was very sad and didn't understand at all why he didn't love me. I blamed him and other people. But today I understand why he didn't love me. When I was sad I couldn't do anything at all. I just let it go. Until I discovered that not having love . . . well, it didn't make me happy, but it didn't make me suffer. Being with friends is best, because in the end, you can only be with your friends. The outside world might think that the life of a *kathoey* is sweet and sour. But it helped me very much. After I passed that storm, I turned around to put my heart solely into my studies. However, when my family found out about my behavior, some trouble started. My mother began to notice the changes in me, and I didn't dare to look her in the eyes. This was different from my father, who didn't say even a single word. I wasn't brave enough to return again to my grandmother's house because I was afraid that she and her family wouldn't accept me as I was. I wasn't brave enough to go and see my old friends from my former school. My mom began to pressure me regarding my choice of work once I graduated by saying that I should become a soldier or policeman. With the university entrance test coming up, I decided to study language further, but didn't tell my mother about this. In the end, my mom didn't object, and because of the score I received on the test, I was able to enter the faculty I had wanted. The change to a new address was something I was worried about; I had to go and have a new life alone. When I had a problem, I would have to deal with it on my own. It was something I couldn't avoid.

From the first day I arrived I didn't know anybody, but I hoped I would be able to make new friends. I decided to make friends with people who were *kathoey,* just like me. I felt that at least we were the same, and if something happened we could help one another and be able to understand one another. My body, my appearance, began to change from a man's to a woman's. My hair grew long and I developed breasts (I used scientific methods to help me). My parents did not accept the way I was changing. My relatives who lived in Chiang Mai spread the news in an exaggerated way to my mother, and she broke down in tears because these relatives had told her about me in such an overstated way for no reason. I was very sad that I had made my mother cry. One part of me blamed my relatives—why did they have to act like that? What had I done to them? This is *my* mother—why is her life their business? On the other hand, I chose my own path, so I can't blame others. This made me confused inside, but later my mom did finally accept me. I felt very good that I didn't have bad luck like other *kathoey* whose parents do not accept them. Some parents go so far as to kick their child out of the house. My father and mother said that whatever I was, I was still their child, and they couldn't sever that kind of relationship. They told me that whatever else happened, they didn't want me to abandon my studies. I was almost unable to hold back my tears when I heard them tell me this.

College education was very hard work, not like school before. I didn't have time to take care of myself at all, and I began to think that

I wasn't able to make myself beautiful like I had in the past. Therefore, I decided to cut my hair short and have my outside appearance be like a man's again. I began to change from *kathoey* to *gay,* as some people call themselves. I didn't act in an effeminate way any more (if I could help it), and I have remained this way until today. School is the most important thing for me now, as my parents have requested. Today I am *gay,* but don't know whether I will change yet again in this life. I pray that one day I will be able to find a place where I can be comfortable.

In my opinion, I've never felt either happy or sad that I was born this way. But I was brave enough to accept it. I really don't care one way or another because I think I'm like this because it is suitable for me; I am not sure if I were a real man that my life would be worse than it is today.

The situation regarding *kathoey* today can be compared to a person standing on the two edges of a boat: on one side are groups that either support us or don't care, and on the other are ones that object to us and speak badly about *kathoey.* I am a person who has been lucky because society has accepted me. My friends and teachers have not expressed dislike in any way toward me. My family has not prevented me from expressing myself. I haven't had problems because I don't expresses myself in an overly exaggerated way; sometimes I may draw attention to myself, but never in an offensive manner. However, when you look at the front page of the newspaper, there are some types of *kathoey* who really overexaggerate their appearance. I am also a *kathoey,* and even I feel disgusted. I can only imagine what other people must feel. I would like my friends who are *kathoey* like me to be more of a benefit to society than this. Expressing oneself is not wrong, but one shouldn't overexaggerate. There was once a person who said that beauty is enough. This should be an example for *kathoey.*

I would also like for society to accept *kathoey* more than it does at present. Don't take a small incident as an excuse to scold us. Why is it that men or women can kill people and act contrary to the moral code every day, yet society does not condemn them? Yet once in a great while *kathoey* will do something to stand out in society, and yet will still be chastised. *Kathoey* are not allowed to study for higher degrees because if they do, people think that it will make our nation's future bad. Yet even if "real" men and women do *bad* things, they won't be held back.

I don't want others to view what a *kathoey* creates or does in terms of it being done by a *kathoey*. That is, I want people to pay attention to the *value* of a *kathoey's* work or performance rather than focus on the fact that it was done by a *kathoey*.

I feel sympathetic toward *kathoey* who have problems and who are still not able to find a way out, who are still despised by society. I want everyone in the world to love one another—in particular, *gays.* If we are envious of one another it will make the unnaturalness of us appear to be a bigger issue. Sincerity is very important among *gays;* if we have sincerity, I certainly believe that one day we will be able to freely and completely become the "third sex" without other people caring one way or another.

For today, I ask only that we live together in society without discrimination. This will be enough for me and all those who are *gay, kathoey, tom,* and *dee.*[6] We should bring the potential that we have and use it as a benefit in creating society. We should make this world a good place to live in, because each of us is born as a human being.

Satree Lek
Third-year student
Hometown: Chiang Mai

"*Kathoey*" is a popular word. For the most part it is viewed negatively. Some people believe that *kathoey* are a social problem caused by society itself. Others say that *kathoey* are despicable people. I think that in the matter of deciding who is good and who is not one ought to look deeply into the background of a person rather than only looking at him or her in a superficial way. There isn't anyone who wants to be born as a *kathoey*. There isn't anyone who wants to be born as someone who is considered strange by society. There isn't anyone who wants to be born to make other people laugh at them. But no one can choose how they are born.

I was born into a family that had more women than men. My family wasn't quite as warm as it should have been. My father did not often come home so he really didn't know anything about my behavior, which was becoming more and more open. For example, I was dressing as a woman and playing with paper dolls. I knew that my father hated *kathoey* very much because I had often heard him saying bad things about them. Therefore, I did not dare express that side of myself for my father to see. I had to say "*khrap*" every time I spoke with him, which I felt was going against my true feelings.[7] I don't know if my father noticed, but I never fully voiced the word "*khrap*" because I felt so embarrassed to have to say it. This was because I knew that I was not a 100 percent man. My father would always tell me, "Don't be a *kathoey*." Each time I heard this I felt like I had done something very wrong and was deeply hurt. But my mother accepted me for who I was, which made me begin to be able to express my true self in a more complete way. So I felt very good that I was able to be close to my mother. The different feelings I had toward my father began to change for the worse. My father and I seemed to be strangers to each other. I felt very frustrated that I had to pretend that I was a man. I had to really force myself to change my character and behavior. I often had to study how my male friends walked and acted.

My father would try to catch me in a lie. He would keep asking me whether or not I had a girlfriend. I would brush off his questions by saying that my first priority was studying because I wanted to get a high ranking in my class. This was the one excuse I could use because every parent wants their child to study hard.

Each time I left my house I would feel very relieved because then I was able to express my true self and could do whatever I wanted. Harassing and teasing boys—these were the small pleasures for *kathoey*. But as soon as I entered my house I had to get rid of that personality completely and begin once again to be a man. I felt very confused.

In the past I believed that I could stop being a *kathoey*. I tried many times but was never successful. I felt tormented. When I tried to be a man, I felt as if I were going through life with a bonfire by my side, with flames that just kept burning brighter and brighter. I became so quiet that my friends started crying and asked me to return to the way I had been before. So I stopped thinking that I would stop being a *kathoey*, went back to being myself, and never tried to be a man again.

I don't believe that men will turn into *kathoey* by hanging out closely with men, but I know from experience that some people believe this. At the end of last semester I went to Bangkok for fun and stayed at a friend's house. That evening I had a stomachache and had to go to the bathroom. On the way I overheard my friend's father say to him about me, "Don't associate with him because he's a *kathoey*." I felt very sad, but had to keep this feeling to myself. This meant that while I was staying with my friend in Bangkok I had to make sure I appeared as a man in front of his father. I didn't understand why society had to destroy me. What had I done wrong? I also didn't understand why society didn't provide opportunities for someone like me. After what happened in Bangkok I gradually drifted apart from that friend. Society had destroyed me.

Although I tried to keep it hidden, sometimes I accidentally let my "*kathoey*-ness" slip out. For example, once while watching a sports game I let out a shriek instead of a "manly" cheer. My father was definitely *not* amused.

I feel very bad about having been born into a society that does not accept *kathoey*. This forces me to conceal my true feelings. Does society know how frustrated I feel? I acknowledge that my being a *kathoey* has made my parents feel regretful. But was I able to choose to be this way? If I had been able to choose, I surely would not have chosen to be a *kathoey*.

Sometimes when I am with my parents I am not able to express myself as a *kathoey*. At other times I must also keep my true feelings inside, for example, during *rap nong*.[8] At first I had to hide that I am a *kathoey* because I did not yet know if there were people who would accept me. When I had to move into a new dormitory I likewise had to hide my true personality because there is a tradition in the dorm that freshmen who are *kathoey* will be yelled at by senior *kathoey,* so I thought that I had to save myself by hiding the fact that I am a *kathoey*.

There were many other times when I had to hide my true feelings. For instance, with love. There are some men who want to be with *kathoey* but aren't open about it because they care much more about society. Every time a person came to flirt with me he would ask me whether I "expressed myself" as a *kathoey*. I'd reply, "If you want to be with me you must accept me. I can't hide my feelings anymore because at home I feel frustrated and I am sick of it." And then he would walk out of my life. But I would give this answer because keeping my real feelings inside was negatively affecting the health of both my body and my mind.

I don't like to talk about the future because surely I have to get married. My father will definitely force me to marry. Whenever I think about this issue I get a headache and feel sick. I don't have any feelings for women at all, so how can I get married? I pity very much the women who have to marry men who really aren't men. How can I get married to a woman who doesn't know I am a *kathoey*? I don't want to destroy a person who doesn't know anything about my true situation.

Every night before I go to sleep I wonder how I can be open about myself without making my parents sad. I've thought about running away from home. This kind of problem has made me think a lot. I care about everyone else's feelings, but sometimes I must care about my own feelings as well. I feel very frustrated since I can't say these feelings out loud. But it's not in my nature to pretend to be something that I'm not. What must I do next? Must I hide my feelings each time I enter my family's house? How can I tell my parents the truth? But these are thoughts for the future. I should do the best I can right now. Even though society does not accept *kathoey* at present, I certainly believe that in the future society must open up and definitely accept *kathoey*. The hope of *kathoey* is to live a normal life in society. And I hope that there will surely be a day when I can tell the truth to my father and mother: I am a *kathoey*.

Tammy
Fourth-year student
Hometown: Phetchabun

The life I did not choose to have.

I was born into this world very happy, but, alas, why, when I grew older, did I have to be unnatural *[phid thamachaat]*? As a child I really didn't know anything about this. It might be because I was born in a country village. My life was, for the most part, bound up with nature. People were sincere with one another. When I was about six or seven I behaved in ways that today one might say were not normal for a young boy, because, when I think back, I should have played with boys, done things like boxing, which is normal for boys to do. But it wasn't at all like that for me. I played shop with my older sister. I also liked to play with dolls, and wondered why my sister could wear a skirt but I couldn't. One day I secretly tried on one of my sister's skirts and put on my mother's lipstick. I thought that I looked beautiful. I don't know what you would call a boy who did these kinds of things as he grew up.

On my first day of grade school I was both frightened and excited. I guess this is a normal thing for a small child who has to go to school for the first time in his life. After a short time, I found that I liked being around my female classmates. At that time I didn't understand why I was like this. I was satisfied by being *riabroi*. I'd get up, walk around, and sit down in a very careful and prim manner. Sometimes, male students would make fun of me, saying that I was *riabroi* and like a woman. There were some classmates who teased me by saying that I was a *tut*. I very much wondered what this word meant; it didn't bother me, since I wasn't at all interested in what kinds of words the kids were using. I just kept playing and having a fun time. Being polite helped me, as it endeared me to my teacher. But in one incident I was teased so much by classmates that I ended up getting hurt and bleeding. What happened was, one day while I had been happily running around and playing, the classmate I was playing with pushed me hard. I suppose he had gotten carried away with having fun. I wondered about it to myself, but didn't openly respond in any way. I also don't know why I didn't tell the teacher or push the boy back. After I finished playing I went home. When I arrived home my parents saw the cut on my cheek; I hadn't noticed that I had a cut or that it was bleeding. My parents were very angry. The next morning they went to talk to the teacher and demanded that the boy who had teased me be punished at once. They also asked if the teacher would mind looking after me a bit because of my weak nature and because I wasn't the type to get into fights with people. The teacher replied that she would watch out for me. This is why, when I got older, I wasn't brave enough to fight with people.

In elementary school I was a very good student. When our class did exercises or things like math problems, the teacher would always ask me to do the questions for the class. I liked English and religion because I thought they were fun subjects. When the teacher asked me to show my abilities in front of the class, I felt very shy. I don't know why I am not confident when I'm in front of a lot of people.

Next came an important period in my life. After I graduated from sixth grade I had to look for a new school. For high school my friends and I attended a provincial school farther away from my home than my grade school had been. It was about eleven kilometers [about nine miles] away. So I went to school by bus. It was a bigger school than before, with students from many places. This scared me at first. Friends from my previous school and from my village were at this school as well. We had been ranked after we took the entrance exam, so we ended up in different rooms according to our rankings. But in that first week I adapted myself and was able to make friends with students who I didn't previously know. At noontime I would eat in the room with my friends who had graduated with me from our old school. Eventually this group regarded me as being a boy who was too *riabroi,* which was something they'd tease me about. But I had a good time. My teachers and friends probably thought that I was just a regular boy who was *riabroi.*

The high school I went to was an all-boys school. The playing and showing off of my friends were very masculine. That is, they'd box with each other and play soccer, they were very daredevilish, and their way of talking was brusque and loud. Of course, I didn't like acting like this at all because I was *riabroi.* That is, in my free time I read books, I spoke with a soft voice, and I didn't like to play sports. The school subject I didn't like at that time was physical education because I wasn't very good at playing sports. So I became more interested in my studies, until I eventually became a better student than my friends. This was the thing that replaced what I lacked in my life, and I was able to proudly be in this group of people and have prestige and be accepted by my friends. But sometimes I still was teased. I never got mad at my friends until some of them became too cocky and teased me too often. In my heart I wanted to respond to them in the same way, but I don't know why I didn't do anything. It probably was because it was my fate.

After school I went home and did the chores that my parents had assigned to me. Things like scrubbing the house, washing the dishes, or reading or doing homework. However, I noticed that after school my friends played soccer or went out to their friends' houses. I wanted to do these things also, but didn't dare ask my parents for permission because I was afraid my mom would scold me. There were times when my mom had me do something, but then I'd make a mistake. My mom would get very angry and yell at me until I cried. I would often secretly go and cry. I'd lay in bed at night and think, "Why do I have to be weak? Why do my tears come so easily? Why aren't I strong like other people?" Sometimes this feeling was difficult to describe. But I had to endure. And I was able to endure until I was successful. In the passing days many things made my spirit stronger, and I was able to overcome different obstacles and teasing at school without having to fight or quarrel with my friends. I had my own private world. I liked to keep to myself and dream about different things. This helped lessen my pain very much.

My last years of high school were very important because they made me know who I was, what I liked, and what my true feelings were. At this time school became coed. That is, girls studied with boys. It was as if I discovered something about myself. I got to know more girls. When I was in a group of girls I was happier than when I was around boys. Whether or not I'd go and eat or have different study groups, I often ended up in the girls' group. I felt that I was one of them and could talk about different things with the girls more than with boys.

My behavior began to show signs of change. For example, in the way I expressed myself when I spoke. My friends liked to tell me that when I talked I spoke in a mincing style, the way girls do when they are talking or gossiping together in a group. And when I walked, I would sway a little, as if I were in a beauty contest. Sometimes when my male friends made fun of me I'd feel shy. It might have been because I had started to enter puberty, so feeling shy was normal. But I was able to adapt to this. And I didn't have any problems with my schoolwork. But what I didn't like and thought was no good was physical education class, because we had to do sports like football, basketball, and *takraw*.[9] I couldn't play these sports well at all. I thought that these sports were not things I had to worry about being skillful at—which was the opposite of how my male friends felt. They really liked gym class.

Sometimes female teachers would ask me about my siblings. They guessed I had an older sister. I think the teachers believed that my *riabroi* behavior might have come from my home environment, that I played with and was too close to my older sister. But my life actually wasn't like that. I'm the eldest child, and I have a younger brother, although he is no longer living. I want very much to reply to my teachers: my *riabroi* behavior and feminine manner in a male body happened naturally by itself. It came from the deep part of my soul. I still sometimes think that it might be because of sins from a past life. My family and I are Buddhists, so we believe in karma, which is created in a past life. That is, the results of what we do in a past life manifest themselves in our present life. From when I was little until I grew up, I'd go and make merit at the temple with my mother. We'd be there a lot. Doing this made me know myself better.

I like to help people; I am easily touched. If I see someone having trouble, I'll feel bad. Sometimes I'll even cry. This might sound funny. I'm a very sensitive person, perhaps too sensitive. I'm sensitive toward different things. My sensitivity brings me strength and makes me do good things. I don't take advantage of other people. I'm grateful to my parents and those who are good to me. Even though anyone can do this, I've noticed that men who are "real" men, for the most part, are not at all interested in these things.

Soldier is a word that, when you hear it, appears quite masculine. Some boys want to be soldiers very much. I mention this because in high school all the students were able to choose different activities, based on their skills. Most of the male students chose student military training. At first I thought that I'd definitely not choose this group because I didn't like this kind of activity. But my friends put pressure on me, so in the end I joined. They had claimed that if I didn't do this program, I would be drafted. And if I had bad luck, I would be selected to be a soldier for two years. This would be much more difficult than doing soldier training, particularly with me being effeminate. Certainly if I got drafted as a soldier I would be made fun of. More important, the instructor might harass me by making the training difficult for me in order to make me into a "real" man. Therefore, I agreed to do the soldier training with my friends. This training took place one day per week, and lasted for three years. It was particularly intensive in the last semester of high school. When I consider what I did, it was easier than being drafted.

The activities were similar to soldier training. We had drill practice and studied many subjects of a military nature. Naturally, I felt very frustrated when I had to go to soldier training. I was teased every session by my classmates because I was *riabroi,* like a woman. In a way I liked it because of all the attention I got; it made me think that I looked beautiful. Everybody wanted to talk to me, and they probably saw me as a woman. Some instructors liked to tease me. I remember the first time we spent the night out in the field. We camped in the forest for seven days. I felt very scared that something bad would happen to me. As I expected, it happened right after I took my first step off the bus in the camp: as each of us got off, the instructor came to check our bags. My friends teased me by telling the instructor that the contents of my bag were more interesting than those of the others. Of course, the instructor came straight for my bag, and my secret was out: he found my perfume, face powder, and lipstick. I was teased by the instructor, who said vulgar things, and my classmates laughed as well. I felt a mixture of pleasure and shame.

I was ordered to stand in front of the group. Then the instructor called the other instructors to come and look at me. Some of them came and mocked me by saying obscene things, but it wasn't anything very strong. Actually, at that time I thought it was normal for men to make fun of a person who has the body of a man but whose way of acting is, on the contrary, *riabroi,* and whose appearance is charming, just like a woman's. When they spoke to one another the soldiers would have to speak loudly and clearly. But when I'd try to use my voice—and I had the feeling that I was yelling as loud as I could—the others would nevertheless ask me, "Is that as loud as you can yell?"

There was one person during this special training period who was very nice and always helped me. He gave me respect. He behaved toward me with politeness, and I felt very satisfied with his treatment.

But there were some instructors who didn't like people like me. When we practiced in their area they teased me very harshly. Sometimes I wondered why they made their drills so cruel and difficult for me. On the other hand, there were some instructors who understood and were sympathetic toward me. They would come and ask me if I was hurt anywhere, if my hand was scraped, if I had any cuts. These instructors would tell my classmates not to tease me. I was very impressed by their good intentions. Finally, I finished this seven-day field test, and everything was fine. I felt very proud that I had done what had been the hardest thing for me. This might have created the strength in my heart that allows me to deal with whatever may happen in the future.

As far as what I wore as a teenager, it was only perfume and makeup. I dressed completely as a man. Because of the way I walked, I think people knew what kind of person I was. Sometimes I'd notice that people would stare at me and then whisper, while others would stare and smile. Some people would stare at me in a negative way. However, I got used to these kinds of things. Because if I dressed like a woman I think my parents and relatives would certainly not accept it. I love my parents very much, so I didn't dress like a woman or do anything to my body to make it feminine. If people saw me as just a man who is *riabroi,* then I was satisfied, even though in my heart I am completely a woman.

I love men. I've been in love many times. I've had secret crushes on my classmates. But I was never brave enough to say anything to them because I knew that it wasn't possible: men expressing love for each other openly isn't possible because society doesn't yet accept it. However, I am able to restrain my emotions. Right now I am studying for my bachelor's degree. I know more people than before. I am not at all frustrated because I think if I am a good person in society and don't cause trouble to anyone, then society probably will be able to accept me.

I still want long-lasting love. I just hope that one day there will be a good man who will love me and understand me, who will love who I am and be able to accept me. I have many friends who are like me. Each one of us understands the other. There will probably come a time when society will permit love between men, and when society will allow a person to be a *sao braphet song.* Then I and all the *sao braphet song* will surely be happy. I also believe that we are highly competent people and have extraordinary abilities in thinking and doing different kinds of work. I think that our skills are the same as those of real men and women.

This is my whole story. The body of a man, but the soul of a woman: a life I did not choose to have.

Thai Silk
Fourth-year student
Hometown: Lamphun

A life I want people to understand.

I was born into the midst of voices that told me I wasn't a "real man." Everyone around me regarded me as a *kathoey* or *tut*. But my parents decided that they would try to turn me into a "real" man by not allowing me to play with friends who are girls, or play with girlish things or with boys who were like me. I know that when I was a child I was much more attached to my mother than to my father, and wasn't at all close to the relatives on his side of the family. On the other hand, I was close to my mother's side of the family, which was made up of mainly women. I mixed with women since I was a child, and was very spoiled by my mother's side. On holidays, if my parents were at work, I'd play with my close friends who had the same characteristics as me. That is, who were *kathoey* like me. We'd play girls' games like shop and cooking. Sometimes we'd play in our bathing suits and have a beauty contest.

As a child, all of my heroes were women, and I always imitated them. They were able to stand up to men. At that time I thought that women were the better sex than men because men only picked on women who didn't have a way to fight back.

Sometimes I played with paper dolls that had many dresses. But my parents did not approve of this, so I had to play with them secretly and hide them. When I was in kindergarten there was a boy who I liked. He became my boyfriend and protected me from being teased. In school I would often like to put on the teacher's high heel shoes for fun. I liked to take a piece of cloth and cover up my head with it as if it were long hair. I liked to wear my aunt's lipstick. Sometimes my dad would catch me and then he'd beat me. I was beaten by my father very many times, so much so that it made me hate and fear him very much; I didn't want to think that this man was my father. But my mother told me that my father did this out of love, and because he wanted to make me into a good person. My mother's words impressed me very much and made me want to be like her. My mother was a person who was neat and tidy and didn't drink alcohol or smoke. Sometimes I saw my father speak abusively to my mother, but she would never answer back. This made me hate men like my dad who bullied women weaker than they were. In fact, it made me want to be a woman who was enduring and patient, like my mom.

As a child I liked to braid the hair of my aunt. I liked doing her hair very much. And my aunt never scolded me at all. I spent a lot of time with my mom, grandmother, and aunt. I felt very warm with them, more so than when I had to be with my father. Today I'm still not at all close to him.

In grade school there were three or four boys who liked me. And I liked each one of them as well. But there was one whom I especially liked because he was good-looking and more *riabroi* than the others. The longer I was in grade school, the closer I became to this *kathoey*. We went everywhere together. He liked to cook and do the kinds of things that women like to do. He could cook very well and make delicious food. He could do many tasks very skillfully. His parents were able to accept who he was without scolding him at all. I wished my family was like that. He wasn't interfered with the way I was. I could work with my hands better than I could cook. For instance, I liked doing needlework, but had to do it in secret.

When I was in the fifth grade both my parents and teachers gave me a hard time. They didn't allow me to meet with my best friend who was a *kathoey*. It began because the school principal went to my house in order to consult with my parents. After that they didn't allow me to meet with this friend at all. Therefore I had to see him secretly without having my parents find out under any circumstances. We tried to meet as often as we could, but because of the situation we saw each other less and less. In the end we just drifted apart. The situation began to become more oppressive to me, and I felt very ashamed. In grade six the teacher raised this issue of me not being allowed to associate with my *kathoey* friend in front of the entire class. This caused my male classmates to make fun of and bother me. I was quite afraid of their teasing. I didn't know why other people had to involve themselves in my life. I was so shy in front of my classmates that I cried in the middle of the room.

When I entered the Tiger Cubs camp I was often teased by boys from other schools. They would come to sexually attack me in the middle of the night. This made me very scared, so much so that I had to ask my schoolmates to help me. But if they happened to be the boys who I had liked since the first grade, then I wouldn't complain! At any rate, they didn't think they were doing anything wrong. They only hugged and caressed me. We were still children and so I didn't think anything of it.

My favorite sport was volleyball. It is often said that those who like to play it are not likely to be real men. I had been playing since the beginning of primary school, and continued until I entered junior high. Then I began to consciously change myself. I was very afraid of teasing and so made myself into more of a "real man" by acting like a "man." In my heart, of course, I was still very much a woman. My classmates thought that I was just a well-behaved young man. However, I wasn't able to cover up my true personality for long because sometimes my mannerisms would inadvertently come out. Once some of my classmates suspected something and asked me if I was a *kathoey.* I lied and answered that I was a man; I said this because I was afraid of being teased.

In junior high school I knew that there were only a few people who felt the same way I did. They were mostly in another classroom. This made me feel isolated. Once there was a girl who liked me, but I brushed her off because I didn't like girls at all. I made the excuse that she was not my ideal woman. I jokingly said to my friends that I liked women who were *riabroi,* and that this kind of woman could not be found at our school. Then my friends didn't suspect anything. I liked doing things with a male friend who was *riabroi,* who spoke politely, and who didn't make fun of me, but when he joined a group of "real men" who liked to talk only about manly things and boast about their status and talk about women in a negative way, I had to enter the group as well. I didn't like it at all.

Some of my classmates thought I was a *riabroi* guy. Others wondered what kind of person I was; they were the ones who liked to tease me. I was afraid of these people and didn't want to be around them. When I entered the eighth grade I began to get to know people in different classrooms who had personalities similar to mine. Some of them weren't afraid of the people who made fun of them because they were brave enough to be open about themselves. This stopped people from making fun of them because it wasn't fun to do. Hanging out with this group of people made me feel comfortable enough to return to my previous personality. I gradually began to be more expressive, although I still wasn't very open. This was because going to the Tiger Scout camp forced me to behave myself in order to avoid danger from my classmates who were not nice. I hated going to these camps because I had to pretend to be someone I wasn't. I had to pretend I was brave and strong, which I really wasn't.

In high school I changed homerooms and made a lot of new friends because I was placed into the "king class," that is, the advanced class. Therefore, all of the people in this class had very *riabroi* personalities. Only a few were troublemakers, but they were less troublesome than the people I had known in junior high. Most of the students in this class were women. There were only a few men, so I wasn't made fun of. All of my friends were women. They saw me as a boy who was *riabroi*. I think they knew who I really was, but didn't say anything mean to me about it. This was different from my family situation. My village saw me like it always had, and still looked down on me. Sometimes my mother would hear gossip and then complain to me and admonish me. She told me to behave appropriately, like a man. I felt bad for my mother and tried to do as she said.

Then I had to do soldier training, which made me have to act like a man again. I had to speak and behave like a man in order to protect myself from male classmates and instructors who liked to make fun of *kathoey*. I suffered in training camp because I always had to regulate my behavior. I had to take care not to let others know what kind of person I really was. The other trainees talked only about manly things. They liked to talk about sex, about their bodies, about masturbation. Listening made me very bored because I had never masturbated before.

My life began to improve when I entered the university, especially because I didn't have to do that camp anymore. I met people who were nice, and more people who were like me. At the beginning of second year I realized that in order to be a woman I had to make myself the same as a woman; in speaking I had to appear *riabroi,* and in walking I mustn't draw attention to myself. I think in these matters *kathoey* do not act properly. They like to annoy boys and say bad things to women, like calling them *chanii* [gibbon], which is a type of animal that calls out only to its husband [i.e., the cry the gibbon makes, *"pua,"* sounds just like a Thai word for husband]. To me, the way these *kathoey* talked about women showed disrespect to their mothers. I tried not to act like this group of *kathoey*. This resulted in my friends not seeing me as a *kathoey,* but rather as a *riabroi* man.

However, it didn't matter to me. I had a small group of four *kathoey* friends.

When I first entered the university I often warned my friends not to go annoying boys because then they will think that we really want them, and that this will make them look down on us. I started hearing the word *"gay"* more and more in my third year. It meant a person who did not openly express his feeling that he liked the same sex. So my friends wondered whether or not I was *gay*. But I didn't like this word because the people in this group were not monogamous. They had sex with different partners. This was very different from the idea—the essence—of femininity that I held. So I began to express my true self and behave totally like a *kathoey,* but I never went to flirt with boys at all. I'd definitely never do that. Actually, what made me express myself more openly was that there was a *gay* person who lived next door to me and we became quite friendly. But then one day he tried to come on to me. This forced me to express myself because I had heard from my friends that *gays* generally aren't attracted to *kathoey*. I am afraid of this group, although there are some of them who I wouldn't mind having sex with. But I must stop myself because I would have sex only for love, and my folks at home surely wouldn't approve. If I act like this it would be dangerous in many other ways, so it makes me not want to do it.

When I was in my freshman year there were different kinds of men who would come to talk with me. For instance, there was this one guy who I thought wasn't thinking about flirting with me, but when he began to make more and more dates with me I began to wonder. But he still didn't say that he liked me. Then in my second year, after we had been hanging out together for a long time, he told me that he loved me. At first I was happy that there was someone who said that he loved me, but after getting even closer to him I discovered that I didn't like him in that way. He still continually sent letters to my home, until my mother and father asked me who he was and where he came from. My parents often warned me to be careful and that he wanted to deceive me. I lied and said that he was a language teacher who was already married.

My mother told me many times that I should marry a woman, but I never gave her a direct answer. I didn't want to have a lover who was a woman because I think of myself also as a woman, so I want to have love with a man. In addition, I did not want to hurt the heart of a woman who had me as a lover. I was afraid she would have bad feelings afterward. All my friends knew what I was, and one day the secret would have to come out. I wanted my mother to know it very much, but I was afraid that she wouldn't accept me, and I was terrified that my father would beat me until I died. But I didn't diminish my attempts at looking for a lover who was a man. I began to look for people who could take me away from my family, like foreigners. Since I wanted to have a relationship with a man, I began to look for men on the internet and joined chat rooms. I met many people, but they weren't the kind of men I was looking for. When I began my senior year I really began to want the man I was waiting for. I wanted to find a man who could live together with me, but I couldn't find anyone. My friends took me into a bar that had men who love only men. I went there very often, but didn't meet anyone. I didn't like this kind of place because it was too crowded, and I also didn't like meeting men like this. It was a place that had a strong atmosphere of people wanting to have sex. And after sex they neglect one another—there are no attachments. Sometimes I thought that I had met the right person, but my friends told me that I wouldn't be able to find love in this kind of place. They often told me that the love of these kinds of people is not forever, but is only for a short time. I thought that wasn't true, that love can occur with anyone—any sex, any age—and isn't only for women and men but is also possible for men and men, women and women. I thought that one day I would surely meet the person who would be able to accept me for who I am and not hate me for being a *kathoey*. I meditated and chanted prayers every night to help me meet the person with whom I could spend the rest of my life.

I continued with internet chat rooms, as well as going to that bar, until finally I did meet that special person. At first I thought it probably wouldn't work out, but he was much better looking than anyone I had ever met before. He told me that he wasn't looking for sex. He paid attention to me in every way and always took care of me. He asked me to go out to eat with him every day. I told my female cousins about this man and how he was treating me. They understood me very well and didn't react negatively at all. My parents felt the same way. I was very happy that I was with him. So I allowed him to have sex with me. He told me that I should be sincere with him, and that he would be sincere with me. I told my friends what he had said. I listened to many people because I wanted my friends to be able to accept our relationship. I even told my parents. He was very serious about me. But after about two months he had to move away because of work, so we had to break up. At first it made me very sad. I cried every night when he went away. Then I started to go out again to the places we used to go to together. This made me think of him a lot. I thought that the love we had for each other was equal in strength. I wanted him to love me forever. I want society to be more open to accept people like me. I don't want society to hate and despise us—we haven't caused any trouble to society, and actually we are able to make society progress. I do not want people to limit love to only male and female couples, but to accept us as well. Then we will be able to be more open and brave enough to express ourselves honestly, and we'll not have to always worry and be afraid of what will happen to us.

I am a person who wants to have a life that is the same as a regular person's. My loving a man will not be a strange thing if society becomes more accepting than it is now. My parents won't have to force me to be something I am not or worry about me the way they do now. I understand that my parents act this way because society does not accept people like me. This makes them fearful regarding the influence of the other people who live in their village. Actually, I think that if something bad happens to me, nobody will be interested, but as soon as I make even a small mistake or do something wrong then there will be people who will criticize me. They will hit me when I'm down. As for decent people who do good, society often does not value them, yet if someone does something wrong society will always criticize that person. But I also think that society will eventually accept people like me more than they do now, and accept us as one part of society, until eventually we will be equal to people who are "normal."

Wanchaya
Third-year student
Hometown: Chiang Mai

The life of sao braphet song.

Many things have happened during my life on the lavender path I have chosen to travel. In the following essay I want to talk about the reason why I became *sao braphet song,* the attitudes I have toward society, the things that I want to give society, and what I want from society for *sao braphet song.*

I was born into a Thai family of Chinese ancestry. I can say that my family is not poor. As everybody knows, most Chinese families are extended. That is, many of my relatives live under the same roof. My father and mother are both engaged in trade. My mother has a restaurant in Chiang Mai City, and my father conducts business with people from different countries and is always far away from home traveling on business. I am the youngest of four children. The oldest is a sister, then a brother, then a sister, then me. When I was still a child, most of the people at home were women, the exceptions being my father, brother, and myself. It was difficult for me to be close with my father because of his job; both he and my older brother had to spend a lot of time abroad. Therefore, my childhood was spent largely around women. I guess it isn't strange that I ended up having some feminine behaviors.

The person who took care of me was my aunt, and my playmates were my two sisters. Up until I was about seven or eight years old I still had not yet been called a *kathoey.* I liked to watch *kathoey* on television. However, at this age I began to hate and fear this word because people were starting to tease me with it. This was because almost all of my friends at school were women, and I always did things with the girls. The reason I did things with the girls was because I was a good student and my behavior was very *riabroi,* so I was able to get along with the girls well. This was why I was always in the girls' group.

In addition, at that age I often received presents from all of my female friends on special occasions. This made me feel very much at that time that I must be a woman, but I tried to change myself because there was strong pressure from both family and friends. However, when I was eleven I began to have the feeling that I liked a boy who was in the same class as me. But I hid my love; I was confused because in my heart I always thought that I was a man. How could a man come to love another man? When I entered a well-known private junior high school I met many *kathoey* who were the same age as me. My first year I didn't speak to any *kathoey,* but I liked to secretly watch them from a distance when they did activities and hung out together.

The next year I began to open my heart wider and get closer to this group of *kathoey*. Because I started to play volleyball I found I was able to get to know them, as they liked to play also. Finally there came the day that was the turning point in my life: a friend who was *kathoey* and I went to see a movie together. This *kathoey* was rather *riabroi* and neatly dressed. On the way there I told my friend that I wanted to shriek. He replied, "If you want to scream, go right ahead. I'll do it too." So on the side of the road we loudly shrieked together. That evening I felt clear and very relieved, as if I had told the world something I had wanted to say for a long time. After that day I felt I could express myself more openly and began acting like a woman with my *kathoey* friends. I started to wear makeup. The first time was for a small party among friends when I was in eighth grade. I began to take birth control pills (in *kathoey* language we call this *"tek-yaa"*). I was fully open about myself. Every weekend I went out at night dressed as a woman. Because I was too busy having fun with all my *kathoey* friends, I paid very little attention to my studies. This was the reason my grades began to suffer.

But the truth came out, because one day my mother unexpectedly came home earlier than usual. When she saw me ready to go out dressed as a woman my mother began to cry. I immediately got out of my women's clothing and, wanting to make her feel better, promised that I wouldn't act like that anymore, but after this the only thing different was that I would change into women's clothing at a friend's house instead. This meant I still had to hide from my parents that I was going out dressed as a woman. However, at this time I was feeling very self-confident, even though I was overweight.

I was dressing as a woman more and more, while at the same time my grades were getting worse and worse. However—contrary to expectations—I was able to pass the entrance exam for Chiang Mai University and got into the faculty of social sciences. Here I received a warm welcome from my seniors and many friends because they saw me as a *kathoey* who is self-confident, fat, and always cheerful. Life at the university gives a person freedom and the ability to be oneself. In addition, many people said that I had a face very much like a fat woman. This gave me the self-confidence to dare to dress as a woman and show off more of myself to the world.

Everybody thinks I have it all: I study at a well-known university, I have many friends who love me a lot, and I have lots of money to spend. But in my heart I am demanding love from a man, and if I can't have it, I can always depend on the services of male prostitutes—who are plentiful in Chiang Mai—for temporary happiness. Today I regularly go out at night dressed as a woman. In my everyday life I dress like a regular man. That is, I have the life of a *kathoey:* on the one hand, I dress like a man, but deep in my heart I have the desire to be a woman. I might have sex change surgery in the future, if there would be surgery to allow me to be pregnant.

I think I'm totally different from those who are *gay*. I am not *gay*. It is different because *kathoey* want their partner to be a "real man." But *gays* can be the lovers of both "real men" and *gay*s. In spite of this, one time I had the idea that I would change myself to be *gay* because at the time I thought that being *gay* made it easier to find a lover than did being a person who dressed as a woman. But what my friends told me was that it was more suitable for me to be the way I was before. That is, I should be myself.

As far as my status as a *kathoey,* I have the following perspective about people who are the same sex as me (that is, *sao braphet song*): Even though society is accepting us more and more, this "acceptance" is not yet 100 percent. Therefore, I want to make society see that we are the same as regular people. I want society to be open-minded and think about us more. I ask that you not despise us and look down on us; do not hate us. I ask only that we have the opportunity to be empowered to do something creative for society. Besides that, I want to plead with all *sao braphet song* to help one another by creating a good image for *sao braphet song* as a whole. If you won't help, at least don't do something unseemly that will only reinforce the bad reputation we have right now.

Alex
Fourth-year student
Hometown: Chiang Mai

The special experiences in my life as kathoey.

My name is Alex. Since I was a child I have been familiar with the word *kathoey* because the brother of my aunty was one. He was very close to my family. But that wasn't the reason why I became *kathoey*.

I accepted that I was *kathoey* when I was in the sixth grade. At that time I still had to hide who I really was from my family. I began to use face powder and lipstick. My mother caught me once, but I lied and told her that I had to buy the makeup because I was in a school play. In high school I was finally confident enough to be a full *kathoey*. When I went out with friends I began to wear women's clothing that I had secretly bought and kept under my bed. Sometimes I changed into them in the school bathroom. The attitudes of my male and female classmates began to improve at that time. It probably was because in my age group there were few *kathoey*—just eight people. This made it appear as if we weren't bothersome to the people at school, but there were some instances when some teachers did not approve. Some teachers were quietly disapproving while others openly disapproved. But we never felt afraid.

When I entered the university I gradually began to express myself more and more as a *kathoey*. I began to perform in the cabaret of Rosepaper, which is a well-known group at Chiang Mai University. Even though I didn't have a prominent role I still felt proud that I had the ability to be in their performances. When we had graduating class parties my friends and I would dress in women's evening wear. We'd invest money in designing a dress and spend time creating a routine to impress all our friends. Doing this really improved our image. I received praise from a lot of friends, including all the teachers who also used to come to these parties.

I was able to behave openly at the university because I lived in a dormitory. It allowed me to avoid the gaze of my family. But then my secret came out. What happened was I had moved into an outside dorm with two friends who are also *kathoey*. My mom visited me there, and I guess everything just clicked for her. It made my mother very sad. I had to spend a long time explaining my situation to her until she finally accepted the fact that I am a *kathoey*. In order to make her comfortable, I explained that *kathoey* are not bad people, but are just one part of society. Therefore, we should behave as good people in society. My mother understood but on the condition that I cut my hair short and not behave too much like a woman until after I graduate. I was able to accept this because I didn't want to make my mother sad. But I still express who I am, although I am trying to keep my promise because it is easy for my mother to find out what I am doing.

As for my sexual experiences, you could say that I had some when I was with the cabaret. After we were finished and got off stage there were boys who would come up to me and touch me suggestively, but it was just for fun; it didn't mean anything.

Now I concentrate only on school. Sometimes I think that when I graduate I would like to study further in a foreign country. This is because I think that people outside Thailand probably accept people like me and have a kind of society that is more open. If I lived abroad I'd probably go back to dressing like a woman again and grow my hair long like the way it was in my first and second years of university.

As for sex-change surgery, I have not yet gotten to that point. But I might take birth control pills to make my body like a woman's, and also take care of my health more. When I'm old I will probably open a restaurant that has a cabaret show. It will give me a place to spend the end of my life.

I've written this because I hope it will help people to better understand the life of *kathoey*.

Waranat
Fourth-year student
Hometown: Petchabun

I don't know if my story will be interesting or not. Although I probably can't remember everything that has happened in the twenty-one years since I was born, I will tell as much as I can remember.

I was born into a family that was rather poor. My father was employed as a barber and my mother was a seamstress. But I didn't lack for much; I had the things I wanted. My family tended to have problems because my father drank alcohol a lot every day and often quarreled with my mother. My older sibling and I could only sit and cry as we watched our parents argue (I forgot to say that I have a sister who is four years older than I). But my family problems didn't affect my state of mind at all. Eventually I got so used to it that it seemed like their fighting was just a part of our normal, everyday life.

I think the reason I am like this (that is, a *kathoey,* although I don't like for people to call me this), is because the hormones in my body are abnormal. I most likely have more female hormones than normal male ones. One other reason is probably because I have an older sister. When we were children I would often secretly put on my sister's skirt, and it's funny to think, but my dad would keep watch to make sure no one caught me! My dad let me do what I wanted. But I can't blame anyone for causing me to have the life I have, because I always knew, from the time I was small, that I wanted to be a woman. Yet, as a child I really didn't think like this. I played with both boys and girls. For example, I played soccer, but I also played dolls with girls. My behavior wasn't hidden from anyone because since I'd entered kindergarten everyone knew that I was like this. It must have been strange for my friends since at that time there weren't as many *kathoey* as there are now. In elementary school there wasn't anyone else like me; I was probably the only one. People made fun of me every day, but being a child, I didn't feel much of anything. I played with my friends who were girls, and I played with boys. I guess I was a person who was fun and entertaining. My childhood life wasn't so interesting; it didn't seem out of the ordinary. Every day I went to school and had fun. I didn't care if anybody called me *kathoey*.

When I began junior high school—that time of life when children begin to become adults—society had become a little more open, but this didn't change my life because many of the kids I had been with in primary school were still with me. Although I still was with my old friends, I did get some new ones as well. I slowly began to realize that I was different from other people. Boys always liked to make fun of me. Sometimes I didn't understand, but I am a person who doesn't ever allow anyone to tease me—I will say something back to them. If someone makes fun of me, I'll fight, but I never start; my mother taught me to fight, but not to bully other people first. I am also a person who studies hard, all the time. So I valued the importance of studying more than how I behaved.

However much I wished I were a woman, my life at that time was actually very fun. I was more happy than sad. In the morning I'd go to school and meet my friends and play with them. In the afternoon I'd go home and be with my family. They all loved me and I loved them. At that time I secretly liked boys, like puppy love. If I saw a boy who was cute, I'd have a crush on him. I'd scream just like teenagers today scream for stars. It's the kind of feeling you have when you're young. I still hadn't experienced true love, but what I knew for certain was that it would be one-sided. I wasn't a woman, so how could a boy be interested in me? My life in junior high school didn't have any meaning and wasn't too exciting because I was still a child.

For high school, I went to study in a big provincial school. I chose to study French. My friend had urged me to study this, and because at that time I was very attached to this friend, I decided to do this. Also, my sister had studied the same thing at this same school. I didn't know if I had made the right or wrong decision to study language, because I was much better at science and math. But because I listened to my friend, I took this path, which has affected my life up to this very day.

I had also been accepted by a technical school to study architecture. Even though I like this subject, I didn't go to this school. It was probably because I didn't want to do the Tiger Scout program. I think many *kathoey* hate this program. I had to do the first level of the scouts in elementary school, and then the second level during junior high school. I want to say that this is the one subject that must be a real adventure for *kathoey*. If a *kathoey* joins, he must be very tired! He must be trained as a man. God, I got really sick of doing it.

The two things I most hated were when we had to take a bath and when we went to bed. I had to be careful because there were horny guys who wanted to have sex. I would try to fight them off, but some-times they would beat me up. Because of this I chose to study at a nor-mal high school rather than at a school at which I could learn the sub-ject I liked, but would then have to continue with the Tiger Cubs. But I almost had to be a soldier again because my mom wanted me to en-ter my school's military training program. She thought that if I did this I would perhaps stop being *kathoey*. But I refused my mom every time, and finally was able to escape from the Tiger Cubs.

When I entered the tenth grade I was fifteen years old. Something happened to me that I want to tell you about. I don't know if anyone will believe me, but I believe it because it happened to me. One night I wanted to go and watch television at a friend's house that wasn't far away, but my dad was drunk and didn't allow me to leave the house. I sat and cried for a long time, until my mom came downstairs and told me to come up to bed. I went upstairs, but do you know what I did be-fore I went up? I kicked the bed my dad was sleeping on a single time. I didn't feel anything because I was very angry at my dad. I didn't love him very much because he liked to drink alcohol and regularly picked fights with my mom.

When morning came I had to go to school. There was going to be an exhibition about the famous Thai poet Sunthorn Phu. When my friend came to pick me up I told him to go without me because I wasn't ready yet. When I finally finished getting dressed and left the house I went to the bus stop, but discovered I had just missed the bus. So I waited for another one to come, which ended up taking me to hell. I call it the hell-bus because it got into an accident with a bunch of cars. I didn't remember anything; I only knew that I was in shock. I could only hear a terrible crashing sound and then people screaming loudly in fear. The bus rolled over many times until it fell off a bridge. A long time passed with me unconscious. When I first awoke I tried to remove the bus cushion that was on top of me. Even though I had no strength at all, I looked for the shoes that my mom had bought me for my birthday. I checked my body to see how I was, but didn't find even a single cut. There was blood on me, but I didn't know where it had come from. It seemed like I was in hell. I thought to myself, "Why did this happen to me?" Then it hit me—the night before I had kicked the edge of my dad's bed! I had done something bad to the per-son who was benevolent to me. So look what happened in return!

My heart was pumping the whole time on the way to the hospital. In this situation, being afraid of dying is normal. Humans are afraid of death; naturally, *kathoey* are as well. When I was in the hospital I didn't shed even a single tear, even though I was more scared than I had ever been before. My body hurt all over and my left leg had no feeling in it. I was afraid it was paralyzed. But when I saw my mom and sister come in I immediately began to cry. It wasn't because of the pain but because the people who loved me had come to give me encouragement.

When I was in the hospital I was shown a lot of love and attention. In my heart I felt this had happened to me because of what I had done to my father. I didn't tell anyone what I thought because I was sure they would say it was nonsense. But what happened to me is a continual reminder that I should not do bad things to other people. As a result of that accident I had to have surgery because blood entered my stomach through a hole in its lining. I wasn't able to walk at all. After surgery I slept for a long time. This allowed the wounds in my stomach and intestines to heal. Shortly after I left the hospital my stomach began to hurt regularly. Every month I went to the doctor. He told me that because of my surgery I was having trouble digesting my food. I had to endure this pain every month until the twelfth grade. Perhaps I've moved off the topic of being a *kathoey,* but I just want people to know that I believe *karma* is real: if you do good, you'll receive good. If you do bad, you'll receive bad. It's all what you do.

Being a *kathoey* was better for me in high school. Nothing much happened. However, I did get to know more people who were like me. This made me more confident, and in my age group it seemed like I was the *kathoey* who was the strongest. I began to wear makeup as well as shave my eyebrows and draw them in. I dressed like my female friends. I was very well-known in my school, probably because I was taller than average. My teachers didn't pay much attention to most of the other students; they were only interested in me and two or three others because we were good students.

I forgot to say that I had been a cheerleader since the second grade of primary school. I did this until tenth grade, nine years altogether. I also helped out by acting and dancing in school performances. I liked performing. Toward the end of high school I decided that I would take the entrance exam for Chiang Mai University because I very much wanted to study in Chiang Mai. I didn't want to study near my house because I was bored with my environment and wanted to see new things. Regardless of my intentions, in my senior year I was very lazy. I think it might have been because I had changed my circle of friends after getting into an argument with them; I moved from being friends with very good students to hanging out with friends who weren't into studying. Soon I was spending a lot of my time worrying about my makeup. Also, because I was a senior, I had to spend time organizing different school music and performance activities, and I felt very tired.

I took the entrance test for CMU, but thought I wouldn't pass because I hadn't studied. For my faculty selections I chose humanities, with my first choice of departments being psychology; second, library science; and third—which I chose because I didn't know what else to choose—fine arts, Thai division. I was interested in the first two choices, but not the third. When I actually took the test, I didn't think I had done well at all; I imagined that I hadn't managed to pass. So immediately I gave up on Chiang Mai and thought that I'd try to get into Rajabhat [a teacher's college], which was closer to my home. Nevertheless, the day the results came back I was very excited to see how I had done. It turned out that my name was last on the list of people who had gotten into Chiang Mai University! I couldn't believe my eyes. Even though I ended up being able to get into only my third choice department, I was still happy. A lot of people in my school looked down on me, and thought I had gotten into CMU because of a fluke. They also said bad things about me because I was a *kathoey;* they said I was promiscuous. But I showed them that I had ability and could not be defeated.

My parents were very pleased with how I had done, but my mother was also sad because she thought that our family wouldn't have enough money to support me through graduation at CMU. I was also depressed, because the faculty I had gotten into wasn't really the one I was interested in. But I was glad that I would be in Chiang Mai, and decided that I would totally change my life. The day my mom took me to CMU I felt very lonely. But I told myself that I had to be strong. My first year I had to get used to my new surroundings; I was very modest and took care to show respect to those around me. I didn't cause any problems or bother anybody. I also didn't express myself as a *kathoey.* I was afraid people would make fun of me, and I didn't have any friends yet. I still wasn't sure how I was going to go about living my life as a *kathoey* in Chiang Mai, but there was something at CMU that indicated to me that I wasn't a strange kind of person: there was a very large number of people at the university who were just like me. It was unbelievable. There were two groups of *kathoey:* Rose-paper and Sunflower. But I didn't join either group because I didn't feel comfortable being in a competitive situation. The members of these groups wanted to attract attention to themselves. I wanted to have a life in which I wasn't involved with other *kathoey*. So I was friends with just a small number of people who lived in my dorm who also didn't approve of the *kathoey* in those groups. *Kathoey* who were my seniors put pressure on me to join their groups, but I wasn't interested. I didn't want to have anything to do with them.

In my second year I gained the confidence to fully express to myself and to those around me that I wanted to be a woman. I began to change my appearance and behavior, and started to take birth control pills. I also began to grow my hair long. My outward appearance became very feminine and matched how I felt inside. This was something I had dreamed about since I was a child. But I didn't tell my family how I was feeling or what I was doing because I thought that they would not accept it. The exception was my sister, who understood me the most. When I went home I would dress like a man; I wouldn't wear a bra. I should mention that I was studying in a faculty [Fine Arts] in which the students had the freedom to express themselves however they wanted. This made it easier for me to change. You could say that my faculty was a great support for *kathoey*. I was studying Thai art. Most of my friends were *kathoey*. There were nineteen students in my class: ten *kathoey,* four men, and five women.

During this time I was thinking over the kind of life I wanted in the future. I was very happy with my life; I wasn't frustrated like I had been in my first year. I could wear a skirt and a bra and wasn't shy about dressing this way. But this doesn't mean that I was confident all the time. When I went to classes in other parts of campus people looked at me strangely, especially those male students who hate people like me. There were many of them, and they looked at me with dislike. This made me feel like a freak. However, I would ignore them or look the other way. But there was one thing which I always thought about: even though I was the way I was, I had never done anything bad to anyone. Plus, I think that the people who look down on us are homosexuals. They are afraid that society will not accept them or are afraid to be open about themselves to society so they look down on *kathoey*. These people are not happy, and lead a life that is in conflict with their feelings.

Right now my life is good, with one exception: love. I was once in love with a man, but it was one-sided. For who can love a person like me? If they do, it is only for a short time. But I hope that one day there will be someone whom I love and who loves me back. This is my dream. I am still looking for this person, but when I will meet him I do not know.

When I am around those people known as *gays* I am confused. This is a new thing that is exciting to be around. Being *gay* is very different from being *kathoey*. For me, there are two kinds of *gay* people: "*gay* kings," who are active, and "*gay* queens," who are passive. There is another kind of person, who we call "bi." They can love both men and women. Then there are those we call "both," who can be active and passive in sex. Then there are people like me, *kathoey*, who dress as women and, for the most part, are attracted to "real men" (*phuuchai* 100 percent). *Kathoey* are not attracted to *gay* men. For the most part, *gays* do not express their identities in public, so those around them do not know that they are *gay*. *Gays* who are boyfriends with each other appear to be friends; only other *gays* can tell that they are partners. When I interact with *gays* it makes me feel that they are very different from real men. I don't know if it is the environment that makes them *gay*. For *kathoey*, it's that we have too many female hormones.

Today, Thai society does not accept *kathoey* very much. You can see this by how television shows have gotten rid of their *kathoey* characters, or by the government not allowing *kathoey* to become teachers. I don't think that is fair. There are still many *kathoey* who have ability and creativity and can be very useful in society. Society should give the opportunity to this group to show the talents of its members before it decides to make these kinds of unfair decisions.

Gays have gradually begun to become more and more open. You can see this on the internet, where *gays* have many Web sites. There are many chat rooms in which *gays* and *kathoey* can meet, talk, and exchange ideas—or look for boyfriends. I think the *gay* community is getting bigger and bigger here in Chiang Mai; there are more meeting places for them, as well as bars. There is something I forgot to mention, which is that *gays* do not like *kathoey* who try to pass as women because they are still sensitive regarding the way society views people in our two groups.

There is one more thing that I think is quite funny. A lot of *kathoey* have changed themselves to be *gay* because of sex. They like having sex with people around them. They change because it is difficult as a *kathoey* to find a sex partner and it is easier if you're *gay*.

If there is one issue I would like to raise in this essay it is that I would like society to provide opportunities for people like me to display our abilities. Do not make your decisions on how to treat us just by considering our outward appearance. We didn't choose to be born this way. But we can choose to be good people.

If I were given a choice I would like to be born as a man with a man's soul. But seeing as I was born the way I was, I have no choice but to live my life the best I can. As for my family, they do not say anything critical about the way I am, but my father and mother still hope that I will eventually become a real man, like other men. I don't think that will be possible. I will probably end up getting ordained as a monk because it is the Thai custom that a son join the monkhood in order to make merit for his parents. Once I've fulfilled that duty, my father and mother will discover that they have two daughters, instead of one.

Mumu
CMU cafeteria worker
Hometown: Chiang Mai

I grew up in a medium-sized Chinese-Thai family with my father, mother, and two siblings. I was the middle child, with an older brother and younger brother; I was in a family of almost all men. The only woman was my mother. I was brought up normally, but I felt that I was a *riabroi* child, and in my heart felt that I wanted to play with girls. I didn't like violence, and was shy around boys. When I began junior high school I had strong feelings in terms of sexuality. I knew I was a man, yet I still felt shy around the older students. At that time my family began to suspect what I was and began to pressure me in many ways. For example, I had to go straight home from school and wasn't allowed to go out anywhere. I felt very pressured and wanted to cry. I was disheartened, but didn't have a way out. Therefore I secretly became a cheerleader. I performed at school. The folks at home didn't know. If they had known I would have been beaten because my father hated *sao braphet song* very much. I was pressured until I was fourteen.

At that time I began to wear makeup the way *sao braphet song* do; I wore lipstick and shaved my eyebrows. I did these things because I was reacting against my family. I didn't understand why they were pressuring me when my two brothers were never punished at all. I felt that I was treated unfairly. I was glad that my aunts accepted me somewhat. I turned to them for advice more than I did to my own family. At that time I felt that I was something strange in Chiang Mai, because when I would go out shopping people said bad things to me, and when I rode on public transportation I was verbally harassed. I felt very bad. I didn't know how to act. When I went out with my parents I had to repress myself. So I was feeling really bad in a deep way. I was very sick of life and felt that no one listened to me. At that time I was lucky that I didn't turn to drugs and get addicted.

When I graduated from the ninth grade I continued my studies at Chiang Mai Vocational College, and I began to be myself. My father hated my behavior very much; he was ashamed. He beat me until I was fourteen years old. The final time my father beat me he yelled at me, "What are you?" I told him, "You can beat me until I die but I will always be like this. I cannot be a man." I said this because I could no longer repress my feelings. From then on he has never beaten me again. In return my family asked me to study hard in school and not to disappoint them in my studies. They also asked me not to get involved with drugs.

After that I began to feel more comfortable, and became a leader in school activities. I was able to do whatever activities I liked. But I began to have a problem with my older brother because he had a family and I did not get along with my sister-in-law. At that time there was a person who came and flirted with me, so I packed up my things and went off with him. After that my family and I began to become more distant. I felt that my parents weren't really financially supporting me; they really weren't concerned about me. So I was constantly thinking that they didn't love me.

By the way, about my education. When I graduated from vocational college I enrolled in Ratchamongkon Institute and studied a subject I really liked: tourism. At that time I was still very happy, but not as happy as I should have been, because I began to quarrel more and more with my boyfriend. And even though I had good grades from Ratchamongkon, I couldn't get work as a tour guide because none of the travel agencies would hire me, as they did not want *kathoey*. So I was unemployed.

Then I took and passed the test to enter Mae Jo University but I didn't go because I was only able to get into the information management department, a subject that I didn't want to study. So I drastically changed direction and became a hairdresser at Sayurt Mall. I know I disappointed my parents. But at that time, if you were a *kathoey* you had to be a hairdresser—it seemed as if that was the only way for us to carry on. At first my salary was very good, about 300 to 400 *baht* per day. I was very happy. I began to grow my hair longer and was wearing a lot of makeup. My folks didn't say anything negative even though I knew that they didn't like it, but I thought it didn't matter because I wasn't living with them. I lived like this for two or three years. One thing I didn't like about myself was that I liked to go out and drink. I didn't save money, so I began to get heavily into debt. Nothing was going right. My parents didn't help me. So my boyfriend and I ran away to Phuket and just left everything behind. My life completely changed because of this.

When I first arrived in Phuket I was tricked by a friend into spending all of my money on taking him out and buying him food and drinks. So I ran out of money. I tried to find work in shops but couldn't because I was *sao braphet song*. So my boyfriend suggested that I apply for a job at the Phuket Simon Cabaret. I was able to get a job as a performer in a show that had only *sao braphet song*. It was a life I had never known before. I was very scared that there would only be vulgar people in the audience. At that time I cried everyday, "Why did I move here?" But when I started performing and my photo got published I found I could get a stable income. Then I began to be overly self-confident in a strong way. I changed from being in the closet to being 100 percent out. I felt that it was a life of freedom because I had enough money to spend freely.

It was a *sao braphet song* paradise because in the south there is much more acceptance than in the north. Southerners see *sao braphet song* as people who are beautiful and admirable. Wherever they go, people praise them. Southerners want their sons to have a girlfriend who is *sao braphet song* because they regard us as beautiful. In my work I met *sao braphet song* from many different countries, including Japan and Australia. They asked me why there was so much acceptance of *sao braphet song* in Thailand. They wanted to know why there wasn't any hatred or competition, like in their own countries. I told them that they saw only the good side. They hadn't seen my life before I came to Phuket, which had been *extremely* difficult. But almost every *sao braphet song* isn't accepted by their family the way they should be.

When I was in Phuket, I had a lot of spending money. I was able to get everything by and for myself. I bought without thinking, and therefore had no savings. I thought I could make money easily, whenever I wanted. I was working, so why should I save money? At the same time I was thinking that nobody in my family loved me and I was alone . . . I felt lonely. In the end I was not able to endure the loneliness, so I telephoned my folks. Then I went home for the first time in five years. When I got home I felt that everything had changed. I was loved in a way I had never been loved before. My first trip back I stayed for seven days. I was so happy I couldn't speak. My second trip back to Chiang Mai was for another seven days, but this time I decided not to go back to Phuket and just stayed on with my family.

I think that the institution of the family in general—or, more personally, my father, mother, and older and younger brothers—is worth more than any amount of riches. If you do not receive life lessons like

I did, then you won't know how lonely life can be. When I was in Phuket I didn't have any warmth. I felt lonely and lost. I didn't have anyone to really talk to. When I got sick there was no one to take care of me. But I am thankful for the experiences of those five years. They made me change my mind about hating my own family, and made me change from being selfish and hot tempered and pleasing only myself to being a person who thinks before she acts and no longer tells lies. I feel that there is no type of love that is as valuable as that of my parents, who still love me. Because when I came home neither my father nor mother scolded me at all. Whatever I wanted to do, however I dressed, they didn't say anything negative to me. In return they actually appreciated me. I want to help my parents as much as I can. Nowadays they have nobody. My elder brother has a job, and my younger brother has started a computer shop. Now I have a boyfriend who is diligent and helps me. Things are okay.

I want to tell everyone that whatever you want to be—man, woman, or *sao braphet song*—we should act in a manner appropriate to who we are. We shouldn't cause trouble to society. Don't think that we are something different in society. We should think about what we do. If it is correct, we should do it. Don't behave outside society's norms. That is offensive. As for *gays* who like men like themselves, if you want to do something you should think over what you will do first.

I feel like I have been a *kathoey* since I was young. But some people have become *kathoey* just recently. They imitate their friends. In the all-boys schools many boys are involved in sex. They have no way to release their sex drives so they have sex among themselves. Based on my experience in school, I believe 70 percent of male teenagers have sexual experiences with *sao braphet song* or with their male friends. So now the new frightening thing is not *sao braphet song,* but men. Sometimes men walk together and we cannot identify what they are. This is different from *sao braphet song*—we are able to easily recognize who they are. When a problem happens, usually it is not from *sao braphet song,* but from *gays*. That is, from men themselves. They have more violent emotions than people like us. You can notice some *sao braphet song* who have very violent emotions. Certainly, they have just recently become *sao braphet song*. They used to be men before. They were not equipped with a woman's soul at birth; internally, they have a man's emotion. When they get angry they show their intrinsic essence.

Sao braphet song—you should lead your life the way you want. Please don't follow what others say or imitate them. Today in Thai society there are different kinds of media. For example, television or magazines have a lot of images of *sao braphet song,* both good and not so good. Please use your discretion regarding which images you follow. Think it over carefully. Now there are many *sao braphet song,* and the majority were not born this way, but rather are being trendy. This makes *sao braphet song* appear ugly in society because Thai society still considers us like a germ—ugly and criminals and addicted to all sorts of drugs. This is because the news that comes out about us typically features *sao braphet song* who are not at all good.

Many people in Chiang Mai regard *sao braphet song* as people who are thieves and sell sex. People here often assume that I am a prostitute because of my appearance. Actually, in Chiang Mai some *sao braphet song* deserve blame because they do not behave themselves. It looks unpleasant. Sometimes I see students acting inappropriately. It was like they were overacting. It looked indecent. They used very loud voices. Some *kathoey* are very aggressive, and scold others. If someone calls them *"kathoey"* they will curse that person right away.

Finally, I'd like to leave you with my thoughts about *sao braphet song.* We must be ourselves. We must not act how others want us to be. Think before you act. Make your spirit beautiful and good. Don't think you have to be like anybody else. Then you will be yourself and be safe. You will be able to happily be a part of society. Remember, if we do good things, they will accept us.

Aom

Third-year student
Hometown: Payao

Before I begin I must first say that I am not a *sao braphet song* or *phuuchai dokmai* [literally, "flower boy"] at all—I am a woman both in body and spirit. Even though I am a woman, I still have heard a lot of things from my friends. When I told them that I was going to write about them and send it to you because I wanted you to understand their lives, they were glad and very excited. It means a lot to them that there is someone who is interested in them and sees the importance and value of their lives. Actually, the most important reason they are happy to give you information is because you are a foreigner, and they want to be famous!

I will begin with Ms. *(Naang)* Gae. She is not very tall, but is very skinny. She is a *kathoey* who is not interested in her body or face at all. Gae is from Nan province. She told me that her family is very warm. Her parents love each other very much; she and her sister have never seen them quarrel or hit each other. Gae told me that she began to feel a change inside her heart around ninth grade. It was a time during which she had many male friends and wherever they went, they went as a group. She wasn't interested in her female classmates; she never thought about flirting or dating anyone, even though almost all of her male friends had begun to have girlfriends. She said that wasn't the case for her. She was not interested in women; she was only interested in her male friends who were cute. In particular, there was one who played basketball well. There were many girls who cheered him on very much. At first Gae didn't think much of it. She thought her interest in this boy was because he was skillful and looked cool when he played basketball. But after she had begun to hang out with him for a while she began to feel that her feelings toward him were not normal, because one day she saw her friend walking home with a girl and at that moment her heart just completely wilted. From that time on Gae realized that she liked her male friend in the same way a woman feels about a man, not like two male friends who are buddies. After that, Gae started to separate herself from her male classmates and began hanging out with her female classmates. Therefore, her behavior, such as her manner of speaking and walking, suddenly became similar to a woman's. She became a very shy *kathoey*. Whenever a cute boy would come and speak to her or ask directions or some other question she found it hard to be herself. Gae would become so self-conscious that she couldn't even look the boy in the eyes. Her hands were so intertwined that you couldn't tell which was right and which was left!

It wasn't until the tenth grade that Gae's parents started to notice that she was acting unusual. For example, when she answered the phone and one of her female friends was on the other end, Gae would slip into her feminine way of speaking. Or sometimes she would shriek in a high voice. Finally Gae ran out of patience trying to hide herself, so she walked up to her parents and told them outright that she was a *kathoey*. She told me that when she said that, her parents were completely speechless. They probably didn't expect that their child would be brave enough to say what she did. Gae sympathized so much with her parents that she cried and cried. But what else could she have done? Being a *kathoey* forced her to act in opposition to her true self. Therefore, she had only one option: to tell her parents her true feelings. As for her parents, Gae didn't know how they would respond or feel. So she had to take a chance. Luckily Gae's parents didn't react negatively at all. She told me that she still remembers her mother's response: "I understand you. Whatever you are, you are still your mother's child." Gae told me that when she heard her mother say that, she began to cry—and couldn't stop! It seemed as if her tears were flooding the house. After Gae told her parents, she became more and more herself. She didn't have to hide and make herself appear as a man at home. She didn't have to do anything contrary to her feelings anymore. This included her relatives as well—they did not dislike or reject her. On the contrary, they gave her more love and understanding than before. She could do whatever she wanted.

Gae told me that what she was most proud of in her life was passing the exam to get into Chiang Mai University. She did this as a present to her parents and to herself. As for her plans for the future, she will probably be the way she already is forever. She does not think she will have sex-change surgery or do anything to her body because today she is already happy. Everyone accepts and honors her and offers encouragement. So that is enough; she doesn't want anything else. Although an exception is money—a lot of it would be nice!

Another person I spoke with is Ms. Ek. This person is a *kathoey* who is very large. We call her "buffalo *kathoey*" *(kathoey khwai)*. Besides her heart, something else she needs in order to live is her daily dose of cigarettes. Ek has had to fight a lot of battles in her life. Her family, including her relatives, does not accept that she is a *kathoey*. Therefore, whenever she is at home with her parents or relatives she must change her appearance and behavior in every way to be like a man.

Ek told me that she has a sore ass because her dad hits her! That's why she must act like a man around her family—if her dad saw her acting effeminately he would immediately hit her. Ek once found herself in this kind of situation when she was first becoming a *kathoey*. She was sitting downstairs reading a book. Her legs were crossed in a manner like a woman. When her father saw that he kicked her until her rear end was numb. Her father is a very tough person because he used to be a policeman. Ek has two older sisters, both of whom have finished school. She told me that she is a *kathoey* probably because of them. When they were children her sisters teased Ek by forcing her to dress as a girl and put on lipstick and rouge. They did this so often that Ek felt she was beginning to absorb this femininity, although she isn't exactly sure when she started to absorb it. Her parents knew she was a *kathoey,* but they did not want to acknowledge or accept her. Her father wanted her to be a man like him, and a police officer like he used to be. Once Ek had an argument with her father and they did not speak for many days. It was because her dad wanted her to take the police academy test, but she wanted to study "home and community." She wanted to cook and sew. When her dad did not allow her to do this she protested by not eating. But actually she *did* eat because late at night, when her dad had already gone to sleep, Ek secretly had food. Since her dad thought that Ek would never give up her fast, he finally allowed her to do what she wanted. Because for whatever else, she was still her father's child.

Ek was under a lot of pressure at home during high school. She told me that her home was like hell on earth. During the semester breaks she wouldn't go home. She told her parents she had to go to a camp. She told me that she thought about killing herself many times, but it was only an idea because she wasn't brave enough to actually do it; she was too afraid. The way out of her problems for her was through her friends. She said that there was one time when she didn't want to go back home, so she stayed at a friend's house for about two weeks. When her dad found out he went to the friend's house and kicked her so hard that she almost lost consciousness. After that she never dared to run away from home again.

At home Ek just tried to avoid her father, until she passed the test to get into Chiang Mai University. Then her life changed, because she was able to meet people who understood her and who were able to accept her. Not only that, some people were just like she was! So Ek learned to accept herself by realizing that she was not the only person who felt the way she did. So from being someone who was under a lot of pressure and didn't talk about it, she totally changed into a new person. She became someone who really has feminine characteristics and is cheerful and fun to be with.

Ek intends to get a good job when she graduates so that she won't have to depend on her father for money any longer. She wants to make her father see that there is nothing wrong with being *kathoey*. Today her life is good, especially with her friends. The only time she is not happy is when she is at home. When I asked her if she has thought about sex-change surgery she answered that she doesn't want to be kicked to death!

Now I've come to the last person. This one is named Ms. Go and is a *kathoey* whom you could consider to be very beautiful. She is tall and has white, clear skin, and a beautifully tapered face. Go is a member of a performance group, so she goes out to work often. Therefore, she must take good care of her body and appearance, and always keep her complexion looking very good. But there is something she wants but does not have: breasts. She is afraid to get artificial breasts. So Go totally depends on birth control pills. She takes them every day after eating. She is always crazy and forgetful because she is drunk on hormones!

Go became a *kathoey* because of her father. When she was a child Go saw her father verbally and physically abuse her mother every day. She saw her mother cry out in pain. Go was not able to help at all. Seeing this happen every day, she began to hate her father more and more. In hating her father so much, she also turned to hating men as well—Go did not want to be a man. So she completely changed herself—her outward manner, appearance, and spirit all became just like a woman's. She told me that her parents and relatives did not accept her at first, so she was very frustrated. But now everyone accepts and understands her because she has never caused trouble to anyone. And she is very grateful. So her life does not have any suffering—except on those days when she hasn't taken her hormones!

These are my friends' stories. I just want to say that these people don't want to be *kathoey;* it is not a question of choice or that they want to be like this, but that it happened naturally to them. In my opinion, in Thailand we believe that we are a society that is open to these issues. That is, we believe that we accept *kathoey* and do not make life difficult for them or distinguish them from others. We feel that they have feelings and a mind and desires just like the rest of us, it's just that they probably have a physical limitation or restriction. However, they are not accepted one hundred percent. There are still some areas in our society that are very closed-minded in this regard, especially in the matter of finding work or being hired. If you have a man's body but walk and talk in a feminine way, don't expect that you can enter the society of those who do not accept *kathoey*. I don't know why these kinds of people don't accept *kathoey*. Everyone is born into the same society and country. We should love and honor one another, whether that person is a man, woman, or person whose body is a man's but whose heart is a woman's.

Thank you very much.

ESSAYS ABOUT ROSEPAPER

Diamond

When one mentions Chiang Mai province and Chiang Mai University to *kathoey*, there is only a small number who do not know of the group called Rosepaper. I will tell you about this group, its activities, its members, and the reasons for its collapse.

The Rosepaper show got its start at the same time as the faculty of dentistry did at CMU, about twenty-five years ago. It was founded by a student who today is a famous actor. His goal was to organize the *kathoey* at the university into a single group for performing.

Rosepaper's headquarters are located in one of the male dorms, depending on which one the Boss Rose is living in. The Boss Rose will choose his successor in his fourth year from among the third-year students who are in Rosepaper. The change is signified when the outgoing Boss Rose hands a gold-colored scepter to the incoming one. Actually, this scepter is now sitting under my bed at home. The Boss Rose is completely in charge of Rosepaper and is responsible for supervising all of its activities, such as its cabaret shows, *rap nong,* and taking care of and protecting its members.

The cabaret show is considered to be the most important activity in which Rosepaper is involved. This activity is the main support of Rosepaper, and has enabled the group to endure because almost all of the group's shows generate money. The Boss Rose will distribute money to the performers, and take out money for expenses, such as the purchase of new costumes or the repair of old ones. This money will also be used for other activities. After their second year in Rosepaper, members are allowed to supplement their income by working at a gay bar called Coffee Boy on Friday, Saturday, and Sunday nights. Their pay for all three nights is 200 *baht.* This money helps the members of Rosepaper afford their costumes. Because of the opportunities this bar gives to the members of Rosepaper to work, you could say that Rosepaper exists because of Coffee Boy.

Rosepaper's *rap nong* begins at the beginning of the school year when the freshmen arrive on campus. Incoming *kathoey* will live at different dormitories, so the Boss Rose will tell the *kathoey* already living in those dorms to gather together all the freshman *kathoey* who are in their dorm. There will be a meeting in each dorm, except at dorm 5, because that is where their rival *kathoey* group, the Sun-flower, is headquartered. Rosepaper members from second year on through those who have already graduated will *wiin* the freshman students in order to make them humble. After this, if there are still freshmen who do not exhibit the appropriate modesty, Rosepaper will organize a *wiin diow,* which means that a large group of members will *wiin* a freshman when he is alone. Carrying his scepter, the Boss Rose will lead his team to punish the student. For their first year the *kathoey* in Rosepaper will not have privileges in the group. This goes on until November [school begins in April], at which time there are big celebrations held in the boys' and girls' dormitories. There are performances organized by both the university and Rosepaper. The Boss Rose makes the freshmen put on a performance at this festival. So the freshmen will get together and practice for it. After their performance, the freshmen are official members of Rosepaper.

Other Rosepaper activities include our yearly outing to Mae Ngat Dam, using the money from our expense account. For the New Year we have a gift-exchange party (most of the gifts end up being birth control pills). At this party some of our members will put on a beauty contest. The first-year students have a small party for themselves. There is also a party that the senior members organize for the students who graduated the year before but who are now returning to CMU for the ceremony in which they will receive their diplomas.

By means of these activities, over time the number of old and new Rosepaper members gradually increased, and the group became very well-known. Rosepaper has produced many *kathoey* who are now quite famous in Thailand's entertainment industry. Our group has produced people of good quality who have greatly added to our society, whether they are academics, teachers, doctors, pharmacists, dentists, etc.

But what goes up must come down. The decline of Rosepaper began due to the inappropriate behavior of some *kathoey* who were not members of the group. Another cause was the "case of the chopped-up corpse" *[garanii gankhahan sob].* It was specifically pointed out in the media that the murderer was a *kathoey.* This made people feel negatively about Rosepaper, and led to a university policy that stipulated that a guard had to placed in the male dorms who would prohibit people who did not live in the dorm from gathering there. Because Rosepaper has always held its organizational meetings and rehearsals for shows on the top decks of different dorms, this made things very difficult. So of course the number of these events greatly declined. Not having activities that included all the members of Rosepaper indirectly caused the group to finally break up.

Dini

The first time I ever heard about Rosepaper was when I was in my final year of high school, during which I was preparing to enter university. I heard about the group from my *kathoey* friends who had already graduated from high school and were studying at Chiang Mai University. Actually, one of my friends had done very well on some test and had been able to enter CMU after eleventh grade. Because he was a very close friend, we spoke together on the phone every day. We talked all about his experiences at the university, including Rosepaper. At first my friend really didn't have anything to do with Rosepaper. But then one day when my friend was eating lunch in the social sciences cafeteria, a plate of food was dropped on the table in front of him from behind. My friend was quite startled, and when he turned around to see where the plate had come from, he found himself looking up at a group of members from Rosepaper. They asked him, "Who are you? What is your name? Introduce yourself to us!" So my friend introduced himself to them. It was a tense situation, but the atmosphere gradually became less so. The *kathoey* admonished my friend, "You are a first-year student. You must behave like one. When you see or meet those of us who are your seniors [i.e., those who are in a higher year], you must greet us with a smile. You must say hello to us in a respectful manner. Do not raise your face toward us. If you do as we say, you will have a peaceful life here at CMU. And if you have a problem with anyone, you can come and tell your seniors, and we will help you." This was how Rosepaper would welcome a freshman who had just arrived at the university.

The history of Rosepaper is quite long. The group was created more than thirty years ago. Older kathoey have told me that the student who created Rosepaper is now a very famous actor who everyone knows and respects for his talent. Rosepaper has continued on to the present day by appointing kathoey who are in their fourth year to be the group's leader, who is called Boss Rose. The last person to be in this position of power was *Phii* Nang because he had a lot of good qualities, including being good at studying and skillful in beauty. Right now he is getting a master's degree in biology and is a teacher in a private school. *Phii* Nang organized a lot of activities for Rosepaper, from appearing at the opening of the dorms to *rap nong* events. Whether it was performing songs on stage or staging fashion shows, Rosepaper always got a good reception from the university students and professors, who thought very well of us. Rosepaper would also often be hired by outside people to perform at functions. I think that when *Phii* Nang was head of the group, everything went very well.

An important rule in choosing *kathoey* to be members of Rosepaper is that they must be *kathoey* who have breasts, long hair, and an attractive face. It is also important that they are not in the closet *(aeb)* or *gay*. Rosepaper will only accept *kathoey* who are open about who they are.

After *Phii* Nang graduated, a new Boss Rose was chosen—*Phii* Jack, who was in the faculty of humanities, the department of mass communications. This happened my first year at CMU. Because I was living with my parents at home and not in one of the school dormitories, I didn't really get well acquainted with Rosepaper at first, because Rosepaper involved mostly the *kathoey* who lived in the dorms. But whenever I had the chance I would join with the activities organized by Rosepaper. I remember that at one of the big meetings for Rosepaper there were over 100 members in attendance. Rosepaper would have activities in order to foster unity among its members, like going to stay overnight in a camp outside of school, or going to a resort on the outskirts of Chiang Mai. At these gatherings we would have fancy dress beauty contests, which were very fun.

Rosepaper had the honor of being a well-respected club at CMU. But the administration of Rosepaper began to fall apart because *Phii* Jack was not as capable as *Phii* Nang had been. He was less choosy about who could join Rosepaper, so people who were closeted, *gay*, or *kathoey* with short hair were allowed to become members. Therefore, the number of members quickly increased. In fact, sometimes a member would come across other members whom he had never seen before. The increased number of members made administration very difficult. For instance, if a *kathoey* were caught stealing something, people would think and say to one another that this person must have certainly been a member of Rosepaper, without bothering to find out whether he was really a member or not. This damaged the reputation of Rosepaper more and more, to the extent that today Rosepaper plays a small role in campus life. Most people don't talk about it anymore.

I think that even if a new official Boss Rose election does not occur, Rosepaper might still exist in the future. But the unity, closeness, and cooperation among most *kathoey* at CMU has decreased. Incoming *kathoey* to CMU do not see the importance of getting to know their seniors, and think they can lead their lives on their own on campus. *Kathoey* from the same high schools, or those who are in the same faculties, will just get together informally on their own. Senior *kathoey* in the dorms will still control their juniors, but on an individual basis rather than being part of something more formal, like it used to be with Rosepaper. Although Rosepaper has disintegrated, this doesn't mean that former members still don't get together with one another. Plus, if someone wants to hire Rosepaper for a performance, its former members can still organize to put something on, like when the engineering and agriculture faculties recently wanted Rosepaper performances at their activities.

Senior members who I knew from Rosepaper found work in different fields when they graduated—some became dancers, some performers in cabaret shows, others became hostesses, and still others became makeup artists. There are also some who continued being students, going on for master's or doctoral degrees. Some former members come back to visit their juniors at CMU, and do some activities together if they have the chance. Sometimes seniors will also help juniors find work as performers.

Rosepaper was beneficial and important in many respects. For example, sometimes *kathoey* have trouble when they are around regular people, because it is rather difficult to make them accept and associate with *kathoey* unless *kathoey* have real ability, for example, if they are really good students or are very friendly. If *kathoey* don't have these traits, people, especially men, will despise them. Because Rosepaper had been such a strong group because of the high number of its members, people on campus were afraid to do or say anything negative to *kathoey*. For instance, once there was a member of Rosepaper who was harassed by a group of men. Within a matter of minutes a group of more than fifty kathoey had gathered to help that *kathoey* chase the men away and make them think twice about bothering that *kathoey* again. The unity and firmness of Rosepaper allowed *kathoey* to lead their lives on the CMU campus in a comfortable way, just like they were regular members of society. Rosepaper also helped to change people's negative attitudes toward *kathoey,* for whether a person is good or not good does not depend on whether that person is a *kathoey,* man, or woman, but on the individual character of that person. So it is with *kathoey*—there are some who are friendly and good-hearted, and some who aren't, just as is the case with real women or men.

Many teachers accept *kathoey* because of their ability to do well in school. Many *kathoey* perform at the top of their class in many subjects. However, *kathoey* still have problems. For example, some *kathoey* who wear the women's uniform to class are still not accepted by some teachers. Some women cannot accept *kathoey* who use the women's restroom, so *kathoey* will have to go together for support. Some *kathoey* are in academic faculties, like engineering and agriculture, in which many people say bad things and look down on them. Students in these faculties think that *kathoey* cannot do well at these subjects. But *kathoey* have shown that they can perform just as well in these subjects as other men and women. Rosepaper has been a support to those students who have tried to enter faculties like these, which were not initially accommodating.

I think Rosepaper will continue its existence. I hope it does forever, because it helps build up a positive image of *kathoey,* which is important for society to see.

Chapter 5

Analyzing *Sao Braphet Song* Narratives

In this chapter we examine the narratives presented in Chapter 4 more closely in order to highlight common themes and illuminate constructions of *sao braphet song* gendered subjectivities. We begin by articulating in more detail our approach to analyzing these narratives. Although our primary emphasis is on the content of the narratives, we also briefly discuss the importance of form and raise questions for future analysis. Although many topics might have been selected, we focus on five major themes that emerge from the *sao braphet song* personal narratives and discuss each in turn. These include: (1) identities, (2) definitions and descriptive labels, (3) etiologies of *sao braphet song*-ness, (4) the notion of acceptance, and (5) narrator motivations for participating in this project. In discussing each of these themes we explore some of the differences and tensions among those who identify as *sao braphet song* in order to demonstrate the heterogeneity within this self-defined category. Finally, we move on to a discussion of possible directions for future studies of *sao braphet song* and more generally of gender and sexuality in Thai contexts. In this closing chapter we refrain from pronouncing any definitive conclusions about *sao braphet song*. Rather, we seek to open up discussion and debate within both academic and popular circles. In doing so we hope to challenge people to think more critically about both the existing literature on Thai "alternative" gender and sexual identities and on the treatment of such individuals in society at large.

OUR ANALYTICAL APPROACH

In her book *Writing Women's Worlds,* Lila Abu-Lughod states that she intentionally provides no formal conclusion to her collection of

Bedouin women's stories in order to challenge the assertion of analytic authority over the narratives. She writes,

> Such a concluding commentary, pronouncing the lessons of all these rich and complex stories, would have restored the superiority of the interpretive/analytical mode being questioned by the very construction of narratives, would have reestablished the familiar authority of the expert's voice, and, most troubling, would inevitably have contained the stories. That I selected and organized them according to the themes designated by the chapter headings seemed limiting enough to their meanings. To have tried to sum up their significance would have reduced them further. It would, in the end, have diminished their power and their potential to overflow our analytical categories. (1993: *xvii-xviii*)

Abu-Lughod's aims are well-intentioned as she seeks out new ways to represent others that will connect people across national and cultural boundaries. Yet, at the same time, to suggest that an anthropologist can ever completely unwrite his or her textual authority seems somehow disingenuous. So although we feel an affinity with Abu-Lughod's efforts, and likewise seek to challenge existing representations of *sao braphet song* that typify or generalize their experiences, we have elected to take a somewhat different approach.

In this final chapter we discuss only a few of the themes that emerge in the narratives presented here. We do so not to look for something "typical" about the lives of transgendered women in Thailand but rather to stress the specificity of experience and to question some of the more stereotypic and static representations of *kathoey* and *sao braphet song* currently in circulation. We hope that the issues and themes highlighted in this chapter, emerging as they do from the life stories of transgendered individuals, will encourage future research into areas and topics that are of interest and concern to *sao braphet song* themselves. Similarly to Abu-Lughod, we seek not only to "overflow our analytic categories" but also to potentially reconceptualize them altogether.

Hence, our discussion of these narratives is decidedly inductive: our analysis emerges out of the narratives themselves, their content and form, rather than from a set of preexisting research questions about transgenderism more generally. It is important to keep in mind that narrators sought to address a very general topic provided by us, the researchers. Participants were asked to write about their lives with the aims of educating people and raising awareness about the lives of *sao braphet song*. Participants had much room to play with in shaping their narratives and selecting which life details to include and exclude.

Life stories both construct and represent the very subjective experiences of narrators (Peacock and Holland, 1993). We are especially interested in the personal narratives as "self-narratives," that is, as constructions of identity and subjectivity at a particular moment in time. Following Peacock and Holland then, we emphasize a "process approach" that takes a dialectical approach, encompassing both life-focused and story-focused approaches. Our analysis is based on close readings of all the narratives, as well as an examination of both content and form. In our examination of content we seek out key words and consider the appearance and/or exclusion of key themes and topics. In our consideration of form we examine the overall narrative structure and "coherence" of personal narratives. By coherence we mean that the text of the narrative has a sequence or order that is significant, and that the various parts of the narrative make sense when narrated (and later read) in a particular way (Linde, 1993). The coherence of life stories reveals the culturally specific assumptions and situated knowledge with which narrators experience and make sense of the world. Hence, many of the *sao braphet song* narratives here reveal Thai assumptions about, for example, the causes of being transgendered and cultural expectations about appropriate behavior for Thai men and women. The internal organization of these narratives also suggests that many of the *sao braphet song* narrators became involved in the project so that they could share their personal stories in an effort to change Thai society and to challenge the misconceptions that many Thai people have about *sao braphet song*.

Nevertheless, our analysis in this chapter does largely emphasize content over form. That is because we are very interested in the specific experiences, feelings, and actions of transgendered youth—not only for what they reveal about the lives of *sao braphet song,* but also as a way of problematizing existing representations and as indications for future research topics and questions. Although we focus on only five themes here, many other themes and issues could have been explored. For example, *sao braphet song* narrators write about love and intimate relationships; school experiences and graduation; harassment, rape, and physical assault; freedom of expression; and community and membership in the Chiang Mai University club Rosepaper. Each one of these themes, as well as many others not mentioned, may provide an important entrée into the lives and subjectivities of *sao braphet song,* and may provide alternative directions for future research.

By emphasizing the content of these life stories however, we do not mean to advance a position that life stories can be taken as objective, impartial recordings of events in the world. Rather, we are interested in the personal narratives as "self-narratives," that is, as constructions of identity and subjectivity at a particular moment in time. Given emerging work on gender, sexuality, and subjectivity in the Thai context, it is crucial that we attempt to understand how transgendered youth, and especially *sao braphet song,* also fit into the larger Thai sex/gender system.

A proclivity exists in using the narrative method to accept *any* given narrative as revealing a preexisting and hence stable and coherent identity. It may be tempting to read the narratives of *sao braphet song* presented here as summing up the experiences of *all* Thai transgendered youth. However, as we have already discussed, narratives are not static creations. As Ochs and Capps argue, and as numerous other scholars have asserted, narratives "construct a fluid, evolving identity-in-the-making" (1996: 22). What we present here, then, are just some stories, some narratives of self that, given another context, different interviewers, or a different historical moment, might look and sound very different. It is important to remember too that these narratives may still hide as much as they reveal. Yet, although the personal narratives presented and analyzed here may simply mark the threshold of our understanding of Thai transgendered youth, they do indeed offer the opportunity for encountering *sao braphet song* on their own terms and therefore in a new and potentially enlightening way.

IDENTITIES

As noted in Chapter 2, researchers have tended to understand gender identity and sexuality/desire in two diametrically opposed ways, and studies of Thai gender and sexuality likewise reflect this binary. On the one hand, such identities are said to be static and enduring. On the other, these identities are argued to be mutable, fluid, and performative. These theoretical positions are typically characterized as oppositional and mutually exclusive. It is significant, however, that such conclusions about identity are rarely based on the subjective experiences of *sao braphet song* themselves. Rather, they reflect broader theoretical trends stemming from the experiences of individuals in very different cultural and historical contexts. Hence the personal narratives included here as first-person accounts represent a vital yet often ignored form of situated knowledge about gender and sexual identities in Thailand.

By providing an opening into the lives of those of who have previously been excluded from national and international discourses about transgenderism in Thailand, these narrative essays suggest that it may be impossible to make definitive generalizations about the gender and sexual identities of *sao braphet song*. Instead, the personal narratives presented here suggest a wide range of possible identities that confound current binary theoretical constructs found in Western contexts.

Some of the narrators clearly conceptualized their gendered and sexual identities as fluid, reiterating much of the literature on *sao braphet song* and *kathoey* that characterizes them as having "plastic" gender identities and sexual practices (e.g., Morris, 1994b; Jackson, 1997a; Van Esterik, 2000). For example, Marco writes, "I decided to cut my hair short and have my outside appearance be like a man's again. I began to change from *kathoey* to *gay*, as some people call themselves. I didn't act in an effeminate way any more (if I could help it), and I have remained this way until today. . . Today I am *gay*, but don't know whether I will change yet again in this life." Similarly, Wanchaya notes that, "One time I had the idea that I would change myself to be *gay* because at the time I thought that being *gay* made it easier to find a lover than did being a person who dressed as a woman." These examples demonstrate that certain aspects of a person's identity may be open to change. With a shift from *kathoey* to *gay*, these individuals move from expressing themselves as feminine to masculine persons, as well as from heterosexually defined to same-sex erotic practices. Depending on contextual circumstances, a person may adapt himself/herself for personal gain, as did Wanchaya, who decided to identify as *gay* in order to benefit from the perceived advantages of that category. In this sense, actors' shifting of identities from *kathoey* to *gay* and back again is a strategic movement that reveals both their agency and cultural creativity. It also challenges Western assumptions that sexuality or sexual identity is the most important aspect of an individual's sense of self.

Yet other narrators describe what appear to be core, essential, feminine gender identities. Feelings expressed by these narrators challenge the existing literature on *sao braphet song* and *kathoey* cited previously. Take for instance Tammy, who describes herself as *sao braphet song*. She comments that she has "the body of a man, but the soul of a woman." Thai Silk writes, "I didn't want to have a lover who was a woman because I think of myself also as a woman, so I want to have love with a man." And Waranat states, "I always knew, from the time I was small, that I wanted to be a woman." That these narrators not only prefer to express themselves as feminine persons but also strongly believe themselves to be women shows that not all *sao braphet song* view their gender identity and/or expression as a mutable entity. Rather, some individuals talk and write about their femininity as a stable identity and coherent aspect of self through time. Quotes from narrators such as Thai Silk also call into question the tendency of some researchers to view transgendered *kathoey* and *sao braphet song* as types of effeminate male "homosexuals" (De Lind van Wijngaarden, 1995; Storer, 1999a; Jackson, 1995a, 1997a), a view that perpetuates mainstream Thai perceptions that conflate transgenderism with homosexuality. As indicated in their narratives, these few individuals do not think of themselves as male or masculine, but as both female and feminine. Moreover, by identifying as women who are sexually interested only in "real men," it would appear that including *sao braphet song* under the rubric of "homosexuality" is not entirely appropriate (see, e.g., the usage of the term *lady boys* in the title of Jackson and Sullivan's 1999 book on "homosexualities" in contemporary Thailand). In fact, Brummelhuis (1999) comes to this conclusion in his limited study of *kathoey* engaged in sex work in Amsterdam. He argues that "*kathoey* first and foremost have to be seen as women," and therefore, in their sexual relations with male-identified men, as heterosexual (Brummelhuis 1999: 121). This problem of defining *kathoey* or *sao braphet song* erotic practices in Western terms resonates with arguments made by authors such as Blackwood (2000), Blackwood and Wierenga (1999), Lang (1999), Kulick (1997), and Elliston (1995). These scholars point out that

Western notions of "sexuality" (including "heterosexuality" and "homosexuality") are not cross-culturally meaningful but must be seen as the product of particular historical and cultural contexts. Hence, when examining same-sex erotic practices in diverse cultural locations such as Thailand, more attention needs to be paid to local understandings of gender and sexuality as well as to selfhood. Furthermore, as many of the theorists cited previously also point out, gender identities and sexual practices must not be conflated (e.g., the common understanding that being *kathoey* also means being *gay* or homosexual), but must be understood as separate categories that may or may not influence and define one another in specific ways depending on cultural and historical context.

The narrative essays presented herein point to more ambiguity than has heretofore been accounted for in the literature on *sao braphet song* and *kathoey*. The stories show that although some actors narratively lay claim to core and unchanging gender and/or sexual identities, others do not. Narrators' ideas about who they are have important implications for how researchers think about *sao braphet song,* transgenderism, and same-sex practices in the Thai context. They also raise inevitable questions for researchers interested in gender and sexuality more broadly since examples from Thailand are often marshaled to illustrate or "prove" that human gendered and sexual identities are "plastic" and "fluid." For example, how accurate is it to view *sao braphet song* as "the third sex," as "lady boys," "gay," or even "homosexual"? How might researchers understand sexual intimacies involving two biologically male bodies if one partner feels she is a woman and expresses herself according to local, culturally defined rules of femininity? Should such desire be defined in terms of homoeroticism, transgenderism, or something else? And what of the "real man" who is in a relationship with a *sao braphet song*? How does he articulate his own desires, both to himself and to others? These are just some of the questions that these narratives provoke. These questions suggest that we might need to rethink the meanings attributed by researchers to *kathoey* and *sao braphet song* behaviors and identifications, and the ways that the Thai sex/gender system has been theorized in the past. Furthermore, such questions might also help us to rethink the way we theorize eroticism and identity more generally in a range of cultural contexts.

DEFINITIONS AND DESCRIPTIVE LABELS

Just as these narratives raise questions about the nature and multiplicity of identity, they also illustrate the complexities and ambiguities of particular Thai descriptive labels such as *sao braphet song*, *kathoey*, and *gay*. It is significant that these terms are typically used interchangeably in both the Thai- and English-language media and in the scholarly literature. An examination of these narratives suggests, however, that words such as *kathoey*, *gay*, and *sao braphet song* are not synonyms but instead may and often do refer to distinct types of sexual and gendered identities within the Thai sex/gender system. Indeed, these terms and their definitions are contested and difficult to pin down, because they mean different things to different narrators, as well as to people—both Thai and non-Thai—in general. In addition, based on their own experiences and situated knowledge, *sao braphet song* narrators have varying relationships with and opinions about each of these terms. Accordingly, readers moving from one narrative to another will encounter widely ranging ideas and opinions regarding gendered and sexual subjectivity.

The flyers that advertised this project specifically asked for submissions from *sao braphet song*, and all of the narrators noted, either explicitly in their essays or during interviews with Andrew, that they currently identified as *sao braphet song* or had done so in the past. Interestingly, many of the narrators felt that it was necessary to discuss the distinction between being *sao braphet song* and *gay* in their essays. The differences they describe revolve around Thai ideologies of gender normativity and sexual attraction. According to narrators, a *sao braphet song* is a biological male with the soul of a woman. It was this local conception of a cross-gendered self-identity that led to the title of this book, *Male Bodies, Women's Souls*. Having a woman's desires, *sao braphet song*, just as "normal" (i.e., assumed heterosexual) women, emphasize that they will "naturally" be sexually attracted to "real" or "normal" men. The desire to be attractive to men who are heterosexual and not *gay* confirms a *sao braphet song's* sense of self as a "real woman" desired by men. Thus, *sao braphet song* will not necessarily be interested in other *sao braphet song*, *gays*, or *kathoey* as sexual partners. This suggests that for many *sao braphet song*, sexual desire is organized around gender difference, much as it is for many Thai *toms* and *dees* (Sinnott, 2004).

Hence, *sao braphet song* are both similar to and different from the Brazilian *travesti,* or transgendered prostitutes described by Kulick (1997). Similar to *sao braphet song, travesti* desire partners that are *men (homens),* not *viados* (i.e., homosexuals or "faggots"). Kulick states "They require, in other words that their boyfriends be symbolically and socially different from, not similar to, themselves" (1997: 577-578), a statement that appears to hold true for at least some of the *sao braphet song* described previously. Yet unlike many *sao braphet song,* who label themselves a "second kind of woman," *travesti* do not want to become women nor do they think of themselves as women, a fact that Kulick notes surprised him. Kulick writes "No one ever offered the explanation that they might be women trapped in male bodies, even when I suggested it" (Kulick, 1997: 576-577). Rather, *travesti* "feel themselves to be 'feminine' (feminine) or 'like a woman' *(se sentir mulher)*" (Kulick, 1997: 577). Whereas individuals such as *sao braphet song, kathoey,* and *travesti* are often held up in both popular and academic texts as cross-cultural examples of some sort of neutral, universal category of "third sex," the details related here in both *sao braphet song* narratives and Kulick's ethnography of *travesti* reveal that gender and sexual expression is far more varied and complex than often recognized. These examples suggest that researchers and writers should be much more specific about the ways that they interpret and categorize gender and sexual practices from a range of cultural contexts and avoid applying Western derived, universalizing categories.

Of course, it is important to consider the extent to which the rules of gender and sexual desire are actually practiced in everyday life. The discourses surrounding who *sao braphet song* are *supposed* to be sexually attracted to might not necessarily be an accurate reflection of lived realities. Thus, it is important for future researchers to examine how *sao braphet song* engage with, resist, and contest these categories and norms in practice. The use of ethnography, as demonstrated by Kulick (1997) and Sinnott (2004), appears to be a potentially rich and productive methodology for pursuing these issues of gender and erotic desire further.

Some narrators also have strong feelings about what it means to be *gay,* and how a *gay* identity is radically different from that of a *sao braphet song* identity. For instance, several narrators believed that *gays* were only sexually attracted to other *gays.* Following a dominant Thai belief that men are constantly interested and engaged in searching for sexual partners, these narrators conceptualized the relationships between *gay* men as being primarily sexual and promiscuous. They judged such relationships negatively in comparison with the relationships between *sao braphet song* and "real men." Such a view appears to follow a more socially accepted (i.e., heterosexualized) pattern of male interest and female disinterest in sexual relations in Thailand. For example, Phi writes,

> The love of *sao braphet song* is different from that of *gay* people. I have some friends who are *gay,* and it seems for me that love for them consists only of sex, without sincerity. I don't like this because for those of us who want to be women the kind of love we feel is the kind of love a woman feels for a man. That is, a love that must have understanding and caring. Sex is only a part of it.

The comments of the narrators draw attention to what is considered culturally appropriate behavior for men and women in Thailand. As we discussed in Chapter 2, Thai men in general are believed to be perpetually interested in sex. On the other hand, "good" women are supposed to remain chaste until marriage and lacking in sexual desires.[2] Only "bad" women—whether within or outside of the marriage relationship—are interested in pursuing sexual relations. Therefore, according to Thai gender ideology and notions of masculinity, *gay* males and their relationships naturally revolve around sex. But for *sao braphet song* who adhere to traditionally normative gender behaviors for "proper" Thai women, sexual relations are considerably less important than emotional attachments.

Other narrators drew attention to important differences between sexual and gendered categories by comparing *gays* unfavorably with *sao braphet song* in terms of emotional expression and personality traits. Notably, these differences conform to stereotypical ideas about Thai masculinity and femininity. According to these narrators, *sao braphet song,* who are thought to have the souls of "real women," possess characteristics such as modesty, politeness, diligence, and responsibility, which correspond accordingly with those of biological women (see, e.g., Darunee and Pandey, 1987). On the other hand, because *gays* are defined as males with a masculine gender identity who are sexually attracted to other males, their personalities are seen as similar to those of "real men," who are often characterized by aggressiveness, irresponsibility, and laziness. For example, Mumu comments that *gays* have "more violent emotions than people like us *[sao braphet song]*." This is because *gays* "internally, they have a man's emotion" and unlike *sao braphet song* "were not equipped with a woman's soul at birth." Interestingly, assertions by *sao braphet song* regarding their differences from *gays* are complicated by the existence of popular stereotypes that characterize transgendered males as hypersexual and belligerent (see Chapter 2). In addition, *sao braphet song* and *kathoey* are often condemned for drawing inappropriate attention to themselves in public by dressing immodestly and speaking too loudly, characteristics considered unseemly for polite, well-mannered *(riabroi)* Thai women.

Narrators also discussed the differences between being *kathoey* and *gay*. In some Thai contexts the label *kathoey* may be used as an umbrella term that encompasses gender-normative males who are sexually attracted to other gender normative males, males who dress and/or behave in an effeminate manner (but are sexually attracted to gender-normative men), and males who identify as women. However, some of the narrators defined *kathoey* in narrower terms. For these writers the term *kathoey* refers only to biological males who identify as women and, just as "real women," are sexually attracted to "real men." *Gay* men, on the contrary, take only other *gay* men as lovers. Thus, the erotic taxonomy of the alternative Thai sex/gender system (encompassing *kathoey, sao braphet song,* and *gays*) delineates who is permitted to take whom as a lover, and in what gendered fashion those sexual couplings may occur.[3] Thus, in her narrative, Thai Silk makes a series of distinctions between *kathoey* and *gays*. First she notes that *gay* men, unlike *kathoey,* are likely to have sex with many different partners. Next, she comments on gender identity, stating that as a young adult she could not relate to being *gay,* which "was very different from the idea—the essence—of femininity that I held. So I began to express my true self and behave totally like a *kathoey*."

Thai Silk also provides telling commentary on the gendered nature of sexual desire that is considered normative for various Thai sex/gender categories. That is, very specific rules appear to govern appropriate objects of sexual desire for *kathoey* and *gay* subjectivities. These rules allow people to find a comfortable niche within the sex/gender system. As Thai Silk writes, "Actually, what made me express myself more openly was that there was a *gay* person who lived next door to me and we became quite friendly. But then one day he tried to come on to me. This forced me to express myself because I had heard from my friends that *gays* generally aren't attracted to *kathoey.*" For Thai Silk, it seems, coupling between people who are *gay* and *kathoey* is inappropriate.

However, it would be a mistake to suggest that all *sao braphet song* view *gays* in a homogenous fashion. In fact, narrators expressed differing views regarding *gays* and sexuality. For example, whereas Thai Silk uses the word *gay* to refer to a person who was attracted to other *gay* men, Wanchaya believes that *gays* "can be the lovers of both 'real men' and *gays.*" Waranat also comments on the role erotic desire and practice play in influencing who is defined as what within the Thai sex/gender system:

> When I am around those people known as *gays* I am confused. This is a new thing that is exciting to be around. Being *gay* is very different from being *kathoey.* For me, there are two kinds of *gay* people: "*gay* kings," who are active, and "*gay* queens," who are passive. There is another kind of person, who we call "bi." They can love both men and women. Then there are those we call "both," who can be active and passive in sex.

These examples suggest an elaborate system of gender/sex categories with specific rules of sexual behavior, categories belied by current theorizations that tend to oversimplify the Thai sex/gender system and overly romanticize notions of "third sex."

Yet other narrators take a less definitive view regarding the meanings of sex and gender labels. For instance, Marco states, "I still cannot completely say what the difference is between *gay* and *kathoey* because there is no word for *kathoey* in English. Therefore, if foreigners in Thailand see people who are effeminate, I don't really know what they will call them. But let's understand that it is a group of people who like the same sex."

Some narrators emphasize that the distinctions between *gay* and *kathoey* also involve how open one is in public about one's "true" identity. Such assertions suggest a duality of self, characterized by the presence of a core identity that is not necessarily variable, which simultaneously coexists with a public persona that may be more mutable. Thus Waranat writes, "For the most part, *gays* do not express their identities in public, so those around them do not know that they are *gay*." Thai Silk likewise comments that in his mind, *gays* are people who do not openly admit that they liked the same sex. It is this ability to "pass" as gender-normative men (who are assumed also to be heterosexual) that makes *gay* men (and female *dees*) particularly invisible in the Thai sex/gender system (see Sinnott, 2004: 9, 29).

Wanchaya similarly conceptualizes her identity in terms of binary components. One part is who she really is, and the other is expressed for public consumption. She writes, "Today I regularly go out at night dressed as a woman. In my everyday life I dress like a regular man. That is, I have the life of a *kathoey:* on the one hand I dress like a man, but deep in my heart I have the desire to be a woman."

The examples discussed in this section raise important questions about the duality of self-identity and the tensions to which they give rise. For example, are all Thai notions of self characterized by core and surface elements, as argued by Van Esterik (2000)? Or is this binary construction of personhood a result of the ways that hegemonic sex and gender ideologies marginalize certain groups of people, including *sao braphet song*? We might also ask whether such dual notions of self are a reflection of historical shifts and/or transnational flows of economic, cultural, and ideological discourses and practices. Future research might explore these questions and examine more closely Thai notions of self, personhood, and subjectivity, especially as they are inflected by global cultural and economic processes.

Dualistic notions of self-identity also raise questions about the contextual and therefore shifting nature of identity and strategic presentations of self. In her book *Materializing Thailand,* Penny Van Esterik (2000) offers one potentially productive way to theorize the fluidity and shifting nature of identity in Thai contexts. Specifically, she explores the concept of *kalatesa,* which she defines as a Thai noun that means proper, suitable, or balanced according to dictionary definitions, and politeness, appropriateness, or context according to Thai informants. It explains how events and persons come together appropriately in time and space. Knowing *kalatesa* results in orderliness in social relations, *khwam riabroi* (Van Esterik, 2000: 36). She is careful to point out that "*kalatesa* is not identical to the English meaning of context . . . but to the coming together of immediate circumstances in time and space in a certain fashion" (Van Esterik, 2000: 40). Using the metaphor of a kaleidoscope, Van Esterik emphasizes that people and events come into relationship with one another in a certain way at a certain moment in time, dependent on an individual's social location and personal characteristics. Any slight adjustment results in another time-space conjunction that changes experience and, thus, identity.

Van Esterik further states that *kalatesa* is crucial for its ability to focus attention on "the importance of understanding surfaces, appearance, face, masks and disguise as important cultural strategies of interaction" (Van Esterik. 2000: 40). Thus, scholars interested in identity might consider the relevance of the local notion of *kalatesa* to the Thai sex/gender system and, in particular, to the core versus surface identities expressed by people such as the *sao braphet song* included here. In any event, the divergent examples included in this section behoove western researchers to be much more specific about the terminologies they use and the meanings given to such terms by both research subjects and researchers.

ETIOLOGIES

Sao braphet song narrators also have differing views about the causes of identity development and behavior—that is, why they are the way they are. Some believe that their identities as *sao braphet song* were fixed at birth, either the result of a spiritual force, such as karma, or a biological influence, such as hormonal imbalance. For others, transgenderism is believed to be caused by social environmental factors such as family dynamics. Not surprisingly, the same reasons for gender and sexuality identities are also articulated by Thai *toms* (masculine-identified females) (Sinnott, 2004: 84, 93-94). The commonality of these etiologies suggest the influence of dominant discourses circulating in Thailand, primarily notions of Buddhist karma, Western pathologizing of nonnormative gender and sexual identities and the idea of a "gay gene," and nationalist rhetorics that frame "deviant" genders and sexualities as a result of encroaching Western imperialism. These theories, not surprisingly, reflect larger nature versus nurture debates (especially regarding notions of sexual orientation) that are as alive and well in the United States as they are in Thailand.

It is important to note that whichever side of the debate one aligns with has crucial implications for the future social and legal treatment of *sao braphet song*. That is, if being a *sao braphet song* is understood as an essential, unchanging state of being, rooted either in biology or an individual's karma, then it follows that such an identity is unable to change. On the other hand, if being a *sao braphet song* is understood mainly from a social constructionist perspective, i.e., a result of social and cultural environmental factors, then it is likely that such an identity might be seen as fluid and mutable rather than essentially fixed, and as therefore open to willful change and/or reorientation therapies.[4] These varying approaches are well illustrated in the treatment *sao braphet song* endure from parents, family members, teachers, and peers.

One influential determinant of people's attitudes toward *sao braphet song* is the linking together of transgenderism and karma *(kam)*. Thailand's national religion is Theravada Buddhism and approximately 95 percent of the population is Buddhist. Karma is the Buddhist belief that the quality of a person's current life is a direct result of their (un)meritorious behavior in a past life. This spiritual and social law of cause and effect clearly impacts how some *sao braphet song* understand their identities. Generally, Thai believe that a person is born as *kathoey* or *sao braphet song* as punishment for bad deeds (such as adultery) committed in a former life (Jackson, 1995a). Accordingly, because one's identity is already cosmically determined, it is neither appropriate for people such as parents to interfere with it, nor is it appropriate for *sao braphet song* to attempt to change it themselves. For example, Dini writes that while at Chiang Mai University, "because I had been taking female hormones, my body began to change. I looked more like a woman. I had a waist, hips, and breasts. At that point the only thing my parents could do was pray; this was my karma and they couldn't change it." Dini later states, "I must do good so that in my next life I can be born either as a regular woman or man who does not have anything wrong with them . . ." Similarly, Tammy subscribes to the idea that her gender identity is a cosmically established absolute that is not open to change. She writes that her transgenderism "happened *naturally* by itself. It came from a deep part of my soul. I still sometimes think that it might be because of sins from a past life."

Biological explanations of transgenderism are more recent and, based on the narratives included here, apparently not as widely accepted (Jackson, 1997b). Waranat was the only narrator who expressed this point of view, writing in her essay that she believes she is transgendered "because the hormones in my body are abnormal. I most likely have more female hormones than normal male ones. One other reason is probably because I have an older sister . . . But I can't blame anyone for causing me to have the life I have, because I always knew, from the time I was small, that I wanted to be a woman."

The majority of narrators emphasized the role of family environment in contributing to their gender identity as *sao braphet song*. This idea of gender development presumes that a male child (or any child) is born a clean slate and that it is through socialization processes that the child begins to associate with one type of gender identity and role over another. Many narrators assert that it was the social roles of their mothers and fathers that "made" them transgendered. Still others suggest that a predominantly female environment led them to model feminine behaviors, attitudes, and identities. That is, they understand their transgenderism—or, more specifically, their *sao braphet song-*ness—as a result of their deep and affectionate relationships with mothers and other female relatives and their contrary distant, nonexistent, or even negative relationships with fathers and other male kin. As Phi relates, she was close to her mother, but never really got to know her father, whose work took him away from home and to different provinces for long periods of time.

Interestingly, *sao braphet song* narratives reveal that they value women and men in ways that turn dominant gender and status ideologies on their heads. That is, *sao braphet song* frequently view women as positive role models and men as negative role models rather than vice versa. Although Thai men are commonly described as irresponsible, selfish, abusive, promiscuous, and alcoholic (and excused for these characteristics because "boys will be boys"), many *sao braphet song* see such characteristics and behaviors as negative and undesirable. These expressions of masculinity are devalued in the eyes of some *sao braphet song,* and as a result they want to avoid any association with masculinity in constructing their own subjectivities. For example, Diamond writes that she had a much closer relationship with her mother and grandmother than with her father and felt no respect for her father, who was often drunk. On the other hand, Diamond admired her mother who worked hard to support the family. Likewise, Dini expresses negative feelings toward her father who also drank, while admiring her mother. Lara, who comments that her family consisted of many more women than men, writes about admiring her grandmother who had the most power in the household.

Ms. Ek (whose story was told by Aom in her essay) views her transgenderism as resulting from two factors, both of which are environmental. First Ek relates that her two older sisters forced her to dress as a girl. According to Ek's understanding of gender identity development, this imposition of femininity at a young age was a major factor causing her to become a *kathoey*. That is, some *sao braphet song* suggest that it is a social environment of excessive femininity that can cause even males to become feminine.

Ms. Go (whose story is also related by Aom) reveals another reason that some *sao braphet song* want to avoid any association with masculinity. Aom explains that Go had seen her father verbally and physically abuse her mother.[5] Because of this Go began to hate men and did not want to become one herself. Aom comments that as a result Go "completely changed herself—her outward manner, appearance, and spirit all became just like a woman's." Thai Silk also tells of an abusive, bullying father. Her father's negative and hurtful behavior "made me want to be a woman who was enduring and patient, like my mom." Similarly, Ping grew up in a family of mostly women and had little respect for her father who argued with her mother. Ping states that she greatly admired her mother's qualities of leadership, diligence, and responsibility, and vowed not to take her father as a role model.

Comments by *sao braphet song* who attribute transgenderism to social causes reveal that the development of gender identity is an ongoing process actively engaged in by social actors. The stories *sao braphet song* tell about themselves highlight the ways that narrators make conscious choices about which kinds of people to emulate and which kinds of subjectivities to embody. Although we must recognize that these narratives of self are told in the present for various and strategic purposes, it would be a mistake to conclude that these are simply rationalizations for otherwise biological causes.

Until the nature versus nurture debate is resolved, it is highly likely that people, *sao braphet song* and otherwise, will continue to offer a variety of etiologies to explain their gender identities and sexual desires. Rather than arguing for one kind of explanation over the other, we suggest a different approach. Researchers might explore the genealogies of such etiologies, the discourses that call them forth, the ways in which they are expressed in social and national rhetorics, including the mass media and medical system, and how they contribute to the treatment of *sao braphet song* by family members, peers, and society at large.[6] By asking these types of questions we might better understand how and why certain etiological explanations appear in the narratives of *sao braphet song* at certain historical moments, and we might also gain insight into how *sao braphet song* make sense of their gendered subjectivities in often hostile and oppressive social environments.

ACCEPTANCE

Although much of the literature suggests that *sao braphet song* are accepted in Thai culture, the personal narratives in this book indicate that familial attitudes toward transgendered children are far from homogenous. According to narrators, some parents felt very negatively about their children exhibiting signs of *sao braphet song* behavior and identity. This may be in part a result of the cultural importance placed upon preservation of family units and lineages through (heterosexual) marriage and procreation (particularly among Thai of Chinese descent; see Jackson, 1995a). Indeed, for some *sao braphet song* there exists intense familial and social pressure to conform to cultural expectations of heterosexuality. In other families, parents disagreed about their feelings and attitudes toward *sao braphet song*. For example, in many cases fathers were adamantly opposed to their sons' expression of *sao braphet song* identities, whereas mothers were relatively more tolerant. Still other narrators wrote about parents who accepted their transgendered expressions. These varied examples make it difficult if not impossible to generalize about issues of acceptance within Thai society, and necessitate a more complex and nuanced discussion about the meaning of acceptance and how and in what contexts *sao braphet song* are and are not "accepted."

As mentioned previously, a few parents seemed to accept their children regardless of their gender expression. For instance, in her narrative Aom wrote about a *sao braphet song* named Gae whose parents did not react negatively to her transgenderism. Gae's mother told her, "I understand you. Whatever you are, you are still your mother's child." This open and inclusive attitude allowed Gae to feel comfortable expressing herself openly at home. Although several narrators also explained that their parents accepted them, it was only on a very superficial level. For instance, Waranat writes, "As for my family, they do not say anything critical about the way I am, but my father and mother still hope that I will eventually become a real man, like other men."

For some families, acceptance or tolerance, when present, appears to depend greatly upon how a *sao braphet song* child dresses and behaves, i.e., the types of femininity and morality embodied and performed. For example, Marco notes, "My family has not prevented me from expressing myself. I haven't had problems because I'm not someone who expresses themselves in an overly exaggerated way." Likewise, Dini's parents warned her not to be "over" (i.e., too flamboyant and attention-getting) so as not to embarrass the family. This statement reflects a dominant gender ideology that places the burden of propriety on women rather than men. Thai women, as discussed in Chapter 2, should be modest, well-behaved, and well-spoken—characteristics not usually associated with *sao braphet song* or *kathoey*.

A close reading of *sao braphet song* narratives suggests that in addition to being influenced by dominant gender ideologies, the opinions and attitudes of some parents are also influenced by media discourses. These discourses mistakenly portray *sao braphet song* as immoral individuals, as prostitutes and thieves who frequently engage in promiscuous sex. Media discourses sensationalize *sao braphet song* by emphasizing their supposed sexual improprieties. In doing so the media marginalizes *sao braphet song* within Thai society, focusing, for example, on their presence in the beauty and entertainment industries, or drawing attention to their involvement in sex work or criminal activities. Influenced by such media stereotypes, some parents seem to believe that their *sao braphet song* children will necessarily follow an indecent or dangerous lifestyle. Hence, some parents seek to intervene by requiring that their *sao braphet song* children at least dress and behave in a manner "proper" for a respectable Thai woman. Only by conforming to such dominant gender/moral expectations, as in Dini's case, can many *sao braphet song* gain a measure of familial understanding and acceptance.

A number of narrators described strategies they employed in order to gain parental acceptance. By adopting strategies such as doing well in school and being a moral person, some *sao braphet song* recognize and take advantage of parental acceptance that is mutable depending on how they behave rather than simply on their gender expression. For example, in the beginning Mumu's father was extremely critical of her transgenderism and used physical force to dissuade Mumu from being *sao braphet song*. At fourteen Mumu told her father, "You can beat me until I die but I will always be like this. I cannot be a man." Realizing the futility of trying to change her by force, Mumu's father never hit her again. Mumu adds, "In return my family has asked me to study hard in school and not to disappoint them in my studies. They also asked me not to get involved with drugs." This statement illustrates well Mumu's parents' assumptions about transgender people being immoral as discussed previously.

Such conditional acceptance may be found among the general public as well, as Thai people's attitudes toward *sao braphet song* are not necessarily fixed, but instead depend on context (Matzner, 2001a). Understanding the contextual nature of social acceptance and interaction, some *sao braphet song* recognize that they have the power to influence how peers and strangers respond to them. For example, Lara relates that she was able to gain acceptance from her classmates by studying hard and doing well in school. Similarly, Mumu ends her narrative with a telling exhortation to all *sao braphet song:* "Remember, if we do good things, they [i.e., society] will accept us."

Some narrators described how their parents tried to "change them back" into gender-normative boys. These examples indicate that the family environment is a potent site for the socialization and disciplining of gender identity, because parents sometimes attempt to actively force their sons into normative male gender roles. For some parents this means involving their sons in physical activities such as athletics, based on the belief that a direct relationship exists between the development of masculinity and participation in sports. Dini writes,

> Actually, I think my parents were afraid that I would maybe turn into a *sao braphet song*. They believed that if I played sports I'd get a strong, tough body and be more masculine . . . My parents probably thought that sports would change my attitude, but that wasn't the case at all—the strong motivation getting me to tennis practice every day was that so many of the older tennis players were very handsome!

Likewise, Phi's father wanted his son to be involved in sports when he saw that Phi did not have an interest in them. Marco's uncles forced her to act more masculine by taking her to play in "dangerous situations."

Many of the parents described in the narratives used physical punishment to force their children to change. Dini relates that "My parents beat me again and again strongly with a belt, and at the same time begged me to stop behaving like a *kathoey*." In her essay, Aom writes about how Ek's parents did not accept Ek as *kathoey,* and about how Ek's father beat her often and quite severely. Aom writes, "When I asked her [Ek] if she has thought about sex-change surgery she answered that she doesn't want to be kicked to death!"[7]

Aware of social sanctions surrounding their gender expression, including the possibility of disapproval, punishment, and even death, some *sao braphet song* choose to keep their feelings a secret from family members. Phi writes, "I had to keep all of my feelings inside. I couldn't talk to my parents about it because they were counting on me, as the eldest male child, to be the support for the family. They wouldn't want me to be a *kathoey.*"

Various narrators used the strategy of expressing and performing their gendered identities differently at school and home in order to avoid parental disapproval and punishment. Such behavior raises the point discussed previously, that some *sao braphet song* may grapple with dichotomized identities and/or notions of self. Actors must carefully navigate between a "social self" that is privileged at home and with family members, and a "true self," which can manifest freely only outside of the bounds of family life. For example, both Ping and Phi write of the freedom each had as teenagers to behave as *sao braphet song* without restraint in the context of school but at the same time having to cautiously hide their feminine identities from family members.

Attending university and living for long periods away from home apparently gives *sao braphet song* the autonomy and anonymity necessary to more openly explore their identities as *sao braphet song*. As a safe environment far from parental eyes, restrictions, and judgments, the university setting also provides a community of like-minded people who may share nonnormative gender and sexual identities. Hence, at university *sao braphet song* have opportunities to connect with an important support network of peers. Diamond writes,

"When I was at the university the feeling I had of wanting to be a woman grew stronger because I met more friends like me. Plus, I had the freedom to do whatever I wanted—there weren't any people constraining me." Wanchaya makes similar comments, emphasizing that for some of the narrators the expression of one's "core identity" as a *sao braphet song* did not—indeed, could not—begin until the late teenage years. She writes, "Life at the university gives a person freedom and the ability to be oneself." Another factor that makes attendance at Chiang Mai University particularly desirable and welcoming for *sao braphet song* is the existence of the student club Rosepaper, described in the final two narratives. Rosepaper was organized by and for *sao braphet song* students and had upwards of 100 members in the late 1990s. Joining Rosepaper allows *sao braphet song* to meet people similar to themselves, and to offer and receive mutual support.

These comments about life at university suggest that age may also be an important factor in understanding gender and sexual identity in Thailand. That such gender and sexual explorations often occur during the period of young adulthood raises further questions about how gender and sexual identities are expressed and transformed over one's life course. Future studies might be more explicit in examining the role age plays in nonnormative gender and sexual expression, as well as the importance of rites of passage such as attendance at university.

The narratives discussed in this section make clear that the social acceptance of *sao braphet song* in Thai society is far more complex than has been previously suggested in the scholarly literature. In order to fully understand the treatment of *sao braphet song* and the place of transgenderism in Thailand, it is important for future researchers to examine more critically how various contexts and factors shape people's attitudes toward *sao braphet song*. Asserting that *sao braphet song* and *kathoey* "are accepted" in Thailand erases the very real social sanctions such individuals endure in the face of stringent gender norms and practices. Not only do *sao braphet song* face emotional and physical abuse at the hands of parents, kin, and others, they must also suppress gender identifications that make them feel more at home in their bodies and in various social environments. Narrators speak of "true selves" that differ from the selves they perform for others. Such dichotomizing notions of identity raise critical questions about the societal versus individual factors shaping *sao braphet song* notions of core/surface identity as well as *sao braphet song* expressions of Thai femininity that seem not only to conform to but actually reinforce dominant gender ideologies. Future research might explore in more depth how the various "selves" of *sao braphet song* are constructed not only in written narrative but in other ways as well, such as dialogue, oral narrative, and performance across varied social contexts. This would require an ethnographic approach with a focus on a limited number of individuals. Researchers might also inquire into the meanings these various "selves" have for *sao braphet song* and whether the coexistence of such selves is seen as problematic or not by various actors. In other words, is the notion of a "unified self" desirable, problematic, or merely a fact of life? Do current theories of personhood and subjectivity developed in western contexts make sense in Thai contexts, and if not, why? Finally, what does *acceptance* mean to different *sao braphet song* individuals? Does it require a complete transformation of the contemporary gender and moral order? And if so, how do *sao braphet song* suggest that such a transformation be achieved? We begin to explore this last question in the following section.

MOTIVATIONS FOR PARTICIPATING
IN THE PROJECT

Many of the *sao braphet song* who contributed essays to this project recognized that having their narratives published would allow them entrée into a wider societal dialogue on gender and sexuality in Thailand. They viewed their participation in this project as a form of advocacy, as we discussed in Chapter 3. The narrative project was interpreted by narrators as an opportunity to raise awareness about being *sao braphet song* in Thai society and to challenge readers and Thai society more broadly to think deeply and empathetically about the lives of *sao braphet song*. Writing first-person essays about themselves provided narrators with a new form for self-advocacy. Using their own voices and individual experiences to challenge stereotypes and generalizations about themselves and their lives, narrators also contest both dominant Thai and Western discourses about *sao braphet song*. Instead of objects written about by outsiders, the narrators operated as active agents creating and disseminating knowledge about themselves.

Some narrators were particularly interested in addressing stereotypes or misinformation people might have about *sao braphet song*. Thus Dini writes, "I want the people who think that being *kathoey* is all fun and games to know that the life of a *sao braphet song* is not a bed of roses. Every second we face obstacles and difficulties that we must overcome." Alex makes similar comments: "I've written this because I hope it will help people to better understand the life of *kathoey*." In addition, Lara felt that the narratives offer an otherwise unavailable view of the lives of *sao braphet song* and therefore have the possibility of raising the consciousness of readers. As she concludes, "Finally, I would like those of you reading my story to think over what you have read. Perhaps it will do you some good." Although Aom is not *sao braphet song* herself, she chooses to write about her *sao braphet song* friends in order to achieve similar goals. She writes, "When I told them [my friends] that I was going to write about them and send it to you because I wanted you to understand their lives, they were glad and very excited. It means a lot to them that there is someone who is interested in them and sees the importance and value of their lives."

The project was also interpreted by narrators as an opportunity to directly confront their imagined audience about stereotypes and negative thinking about transgendered people. These *sao braphet song* use their essays to contest what they feel are ignorant and unjust attitudes. Ping admonishes, "Stop! Stop looking down on and despising the third sex! The third sex are born as human beings, just like other people. They have the same status and freedom of being human just as others do. Give a chance to the third sex."

In some cases, the essays served as a forum in which narrators could deliver messages directly to other *sao braphet song* about moral behavior, gender performance, and social acceptance. For example, recall Mumu's caution to other *sao braphet song,* "Think before you act. . . . Remember, if we do good things, they [i.e., society] will accept us." Wanchaya likewise writes, "I want to plead with all *sao braphet song* to help one another by creating a good image for *sao braphet song* as a whole. If you won't help, at least don't do something unseemly that will only reinforce the bad reputation we have right now." Such comments suggest that advocacy and transformation must first begin with the self and a critical look at one's own behavior. Yet at the same time these statements also raise important questions about the ways that morality in the Thai context is intimately bound up with appearance and conformity. Furthermore, these comments suggest group identity formation and internal group boundary maintenance, aspects of *sao braphet song* lives that have not yet been studied.

Beyond making appeals to Thai and Western audiences to better understand their lives, *sao braphet song* narrators also incorporated into their essays demands for social transformation and personal empowerment. Specifically, actors wrote about the need for Thai to change the way they think about and treat *sao braphet song.* They write about inclusion and exclusion and about discrimination in the workplace, asserting that discrimination prevents *sao braphet song* from positively contributing to society. They remind readers that they have much to offer. Wanchaya states, "I want society to be open-minded and think about us more. I ask that you not despise us and look down on us; do not hate us. I ask only that we have the opportunity to be empowered to do something creative for society." Marco makes a similar appeal and focuses on discrimination against those who express nonnormative gender identities. She writes, "For today, I ask only that we live together in society without discrimination. This will be enough for me and all those who are *gay, kathoey, tom,* and *dee.* We should bring the potential that we have and use it as a benefit in creating society. We should make this world a good place to live in, because each of us is born as a human being." Waranat, too, comments on the limitations faced by *sao braphet song,* "If there is one issue I would like to raise in this essay it is that I would like society to provide opportunities for people like me to display our abilities. Do not make your decisions on how to treat us just by considering our outward appearance. We didn't choose to be born this way. But we can choose to be good people."

Waranat's demand seeks not only to create new opportunities for *sao braphet song* to contribute to society, but also to create new ways of thinking about *sao braphet song* as moral individuals and crucial members of society. By criticizing a focus on "outward appearance," Waranat's comments go to the heart of the problem for *sao braphet song.* That is, gender ideology is so deeply entrenched in Thailand (as well as around the world) that anyone who transcends the "normal" boundaries of sex and gender is instantly ostracized and disciplined into submission, or, alternatively, is marginalized into nonexistence. Waranat's comments, although they assert an essentialist notion of *sao braphet song* identity ("we didn't choose to be born this way"), emphasize that despite biology, past karma, or outward presentations of self that *sao braphet song* "can choose to be good people," i.e., to be moral persons who positively contribute to Thai society. To persuade readers of that idea would be to challenge and transform the very foundations of the Thai social order. It would result in a society in which *sao braphet song* are no longer seen as "other" but as integral and celebrated parts of Thai society. Aom's comments about her *sao braphet song* friends are apropos here. She concludes her essay thus, "Everyone is born into the same society and country. We should love and honor one another, whether that person is a man, woman, or a person whose body is a man's but whose heart is a woman's."

WHERE TO GO FROM HERE

Our goals in this chapter have been twofold, and are directly related to our vision for future study and understanding of *sao braphet song*. First, in our analysis of *sao braphet song* narratives we wanted to demonstrate the heterogeneity of *sao braphet song* subjectivities and experiences as a means of problematizing what is now taken-for-granted knowledge about gender and sexuality, and specifically transgenderism, in Thailand. By juxtaposing the essays against one another and drawing out both the differences and similarities in *sao braphet song* narratives of self, we have endeavored to challenge existing misinformation and misinterpretation, both at the level of scholarship and at the level of everyday social interaction in Thailand. Second, we wanted to open up further dialogue about these issues by posing interesting and provocative questions. The questions we offer throughout this chapter have various purposes: sometimes to shift the perspective of the reader or analyst, sometimes to unearth hidden assumptions in current thinking, sometimes to expose faulty logic or theoretical assertions based on conjecture rather than concrete ethnographic examples. Most important, we want to avoid any neat and tidy presentation of *sao braphet song*-ness.

Although what we leave here may seem unfinished, it is precisely this disorder and inchoateness that we seek to privilege. For as scholars of the narrative method have emphasized over and over again, and as we have painstakingly tried to reiterate here, personal narratives are fluid identities-in-the-making, perpetually contingent, ever changing and evolving (Ochs and Capps, 1996). They transform with time, context, listener, and research encounter. As such, the narratives published in this book do in some ways reify *sao braphet song* and threaten to fix them in time and space. Yet we feel this project is worth the risk—and it seems from contributors' comments that they do as well. Personal narratives make plain how individuals make sense of their lives, how they experience/reflect on the world, and how they actively negotiate social norms and ideologies that marginalize their existence—even if only momentarily. If our ultimate goal is to understand what it means to people to be *sao braphet song,* and, more specifically, what it means to be "a woman's soul in a man's body," then personal narratives seem an appropriate place to begin.

Notes

Chapter One

1. For example, scholar Peter Jackson has contributed the most to our understanding of nonnormative sexual behavior and identity in Thailand. He typically employs the terms *kathoey* (e.g., 1995a; 1997a) and *lady boy* (Jackson and Sullivan, 1999) when referring to biological men who transgress normative gender boundaries and appear "effeminate." The main problem with the term *lady boy* is that it is frequently used by non-Thai to refer to cross-dressing prostitutes. See, e.g., Woodward (2002) and the documentary films *Ladyboys* (1992), dir. Jeremy Marre, and *Ladyboy Story* (1998), dir. Jane Snijder.

2. Sinnott (2004), Jackson (1995a), and Morris (1994b) note that in the past the term *kathoey* was also used to refer to women who transgressed normative gender boundaries, and the term is occasionally still applied to women today (Sinnott, 2004: 59). We have chosen to use the term *sao braphet song* as a way of limiting our frame of reference to men who, to varying degrees, present themselves as women.

3. Those interested in the politics surrounding the term *transgender* may consult the special issue of the *International Journal of Transgenderism*: "What Is Transgender?" volume 4, number 3, July-September 2000.

4. For example, when mentioning the lavish historical film *Suriyothai* (2001) to our Thai friends, we were frequently told that its Thai costume designer, Kamol Panitpan, was *"kathoey."*

5. In this book we make a clear distinction between the terms *sex* and *gender.* Sex is a biological category of difference based on genitalia, physiology, and/or genetics that distinguishes "male" from "female." Gender is a social and cultural category of difference that divides people into men and women, masculine and feminine. Although categories of both sex and gender are increasingly understood by feminists and social scientists as culturally and socially constructed and historically situated, a tendency still exists for the general public (both in the United States and Thailand) to assume that sex is a "natural" and given category, and that sex and gender are isomorphic in "normal" individuals (i.e., bodies with penises [males] are automatically men and express a masculine gender). The title of our book, *Male Bodies, Women's Souls* seeks to play on general understandings of these categories and to point to the types of gender crossings engaged in by *sao braphet song.*

Male Bodies, Women's Souls
© 2007 by The Haworth Press, Inc. All rights reserved.
doi:10.1300/5750_06

6. Although some Thai women cross socially approved gender boundaries (see, e.g., Sinnott, 2004, 1999), we limit our discussion to *sao braphet song* (i.e., males who express themselves and/or identify as women).

7. See hate crime statistics and reports at http://www.lambda.org.

8. It should be noted that the English term *homosexual* may not map neatly onto the lived realities and meanings of sexual behavior between Thai individuals, hence the term is used only provisionally. See Blackwood (2000), Blackwood and Wieringa (1999), Lang (1999), Kulick (1997), Elliston (1995), and Weston (1993) for critical reflections on the application to non-Western cultural contexts of culturally specific terms describing erotic practices and desires. This issue is addressed further in Chapter 5.

9. Biographies and autobiographies of transgendered individuals in western contexts include Martino (1977), Bornstein (1994), RuPaul (1995), Von Mahlsdorf (1995), Pettiway (1996), Rees (1996), Devor (1997), Gorman (1998), McCloskey (2000), Jorgensen and Stryker (2000), Brevard (2001), and Matzner (2001).

10. We address this issue in more detail in Chapter 5. See, for example, Brummelheis (1999), who argues that *kathoey* should be considered "women" rather than "male homosexuals."

11. White (2000) and Riessman (1993) note that the narrative method can be engaged in multiple and varied ways. We feel that such diversity is a strength rather than a hindrance.

12. Our decision about the book's organization and lack of a concluding chapter was influenced by Lila Abu-Lughod's thoughtful and innovative book *Writing Women's Worlds* (1993).

Chapter Two

1. Similar to the term *homosexual* referred to in footnote 8 in Chapter 1, the term *heterosexual* should also be viewed critically when used to speak about sexual practices and identities in Thai contexts since the meaning of this term varies as one moves across cultural and national borders.

2. Because the English word *gay* has been incorporated into the Thai language and has culturally specific meanings, we use italics to signify when it should be understood as occurring in the Thai context.

3. On India, see O'Flaherty (1980) and Nanda (1999); on Burma, see Spiro (1967) and Coleman, Cogan, and Gooren (1992); on Malaysia, see Teh (1998).

4. Usage of the term *hermaphrodite* raises questions about translation and meaning. In English, the term has been used historically to refer to individuals born with a combination of male and female external genitalia, gonads, and/or chromosomes. In the 1990s the term hermaphrodite was challenged by those individuals who had previously been defined as such since the term is based on misleading notions of "true sex" and is highly stigmatizing. Today the label *intersex* is advocated as a replacement for hermaphrodite (see http://www.isna.org). In analyzing sex and gender in the Thai context, the terms *hermaphrodite* and *kathoey* have often been used interchangeably. However, *hermaphrodite* typically refers to sexual characteristics, whereas *kathoey*, at least in contemporary usage, typically refers to gender characteristics, hence references to hermaphrodites and/or *kathoey* in historical nar-

ratives should be more carefully analyzed for their political implications in the present. See Sinnott (2004: 5) for a slightly different explanation of the terms *hermaphrodite* and *kathoey*.

5. Although first reprinted in 1965, and then in 1991, the date of the original printing of *Consul in Paradise* appears to be unknown. Wood notes that this book "was originally published in Bangkok, Siam, some time before World War II. During the war the premises of the press where it was printed were destroyed by a British bomb, and most of the copies of the book then in stock, as well as all the blocks for the illustrations, were lost" (*xi*).

6. For a rather different interpretation of *kathoey*, mediumship, and performativity, see Morris (2000: 128-134).

7. Terms used in the Thai press to describe such students included: *kathoey*, *gay*, *tut* (a derogatory word similar to "faggot" in English), *tom* (a masculine-identified lesbian), and *dee* (a feminine-identified lesbian) (see, Anonymous, 1996a,b). Apparently a ban on transgendered and homosexual individuals had already been implemented by the Rajabhat Institute on a "limited and selective basis" beginning in 1993 but had never before been publicized (Anonymous 1997b).

8. Such films include *Saving Private Tootsie* (2002, dir. Kittikorn Liasirikun); *Iron Ladies 2: Before and After* (2003, dir. Youngyoot Thongkongtoon); and *Beautiful Boxer* (2003, dir. Eakachai Uekrongtham).

9. But see Winter (2002) for research on gender-trait stereotypes.

Chapter Three

1. This is Langness and Frank's term and reflects the language of the time. We personally take issue with characterizing those who do not conform to dominant social values and beliefs as "deviant."

2. This is referred to in the literature as a *phenomenological approach*. See Watson and Watson-Franke (1985).

3. Readers interested in the anthropological literature on self might begin with the review article by Ochs and Capps (1996) and the numerous publications cited therein.

4. Also see Caplan (1997: 12-13) and Behar (1993: 347, fn 16) for discussions of other key feminist works.

5. Although the term *marginal* certainly seems apropos to the situation of *sao braphet song* in Thailand, scholars in the Personal Narratives Group remind us that the meaning of marginality may be problematic, particularly when used by first world people to describe third-world contexts (1989: 11). They assert that the term can assume an imperialist and colonialist point of view. Those we label *marginal* may not necessarily define themselves as such and, in fact, such a "deviation from the norm" could be seen as empowering (Personal Narratives Group, 1989: 11). Hence, we use the term *marginal* with caution.

Similarly, it is also important to note, as we discuss in Chapter 2, that specific contexts do exist in Thai society in which transgendered people (i.e., spirit mediums) are valued, rather than marginalized. Hence, it is important to note the contingent, context-based meaning of gender identity in Thailand and elsewhere.

Chapter Four

1. Contributors' names have been changed and in some instances, additional identifying personal information has been removed to protect the privacy of participants in this project.

2. *Lan Na* means "one thousand rice fields" in Thai and is more commonly written in English as *Lanna.*

3. For some contributors, the phrase *riabroi,* with its meaning of being well-mannered and neatly dressed, was more associated with femininity than masculinity.

4. *Phii* is used as a title of respect to indicate the senior person in a relationship.

5. In Thailand volleyball is stereotyped as a girls' rather than boys' sport.

6. *Tom* (from the English "tomboy") refers to masculine-identified lesbians, whereas *dee* is used to refer to lesbians who dress and behave in a feminine manner.

7. *Khrap* is a sentence-ending particle used by male Thai speakers for politeness purposes; women (and *kathoey*) use *kha.*

8. *Rap nong,* literally "receiving the juniors," refers to freshmen hazing activities at Chiang Mai University. Such hazing of all first-year students occurs at other Thai universities and high schools as well.

9. *Takraw* is a sport similar to volleyball, played with a small rattan ball, in which any part of the body except the hands can be used to hit the ball over a net.

Chapter Five

1. We use the word *actors* instead of *subjects,* which can be taken in a pejorative sense that fails to recognize the agency and creativity of human beings.

2. For example, Warunee discusses the ways that young Thai girls are socialized to view sex as "forbidden, dirty and shameful" and to consider discussion of sexual matters "indecent and dirty" (2002: 160).

3. This erotic taxonomy is not unlike those found in certain Native American cultures, as described and analyzed by Lang (1999). She notes which sorts of couplings and relationships are "culturally acknowledged, accepted and sanctioned" (Lang, 1999: 98).

4. See Murray (1992) for an enlightening yet disturbing description of reorientation therapies utilized in Western countries over the past two centuries for those exhibiting gender and sexual "deviance."

5. These comments raise the issue of domestic violence, which has historically been a taboo subject in Thai society. Recent work reveals that domestic violence is a significant problem, especially for Thai women. See, e.g., Costa and Matzner (2002), Maytinee Bhongsavej and Suteera Thomson Vichitranonda (2001), Suteera Thomson Vichitranonda and Maytinee Bhongsavej (2001), Voices of Thai Women (1997).

6. Both Jackson and Sinnott have done work in this area, focusing mainly on *gay* males (Jackson 1997b), and *toms* and *dees* (Sinnott, 2004).

7. It should be noted that kicking is a very negative act in Thai culture, usually associated with human treatment of animals (especially dogs) rather than humans.

Hence, to kick one's own son to death suggests extreme rage and hatred, possibly toward what is perceived as excessively immoral behavior. Although it is possible that Ek made this comment sarcastically or humorously, it pointedly reveals the extremely negative emotions and behaviors provoked by those who challenge normative gender practice.

Bibliography

Abu-Lughod, L. 1990. Can There Be a Feminist Ethnography? *Women and Performance: A Journal of Feminist Theory* 5(1), 7-27.

Abu-Lughod, L. 1993. *Writing Women's Worlds*. Berkeley: University of California Press.

Anonymous. 1996a. Dress Up and Play the Game. *The Economist,* July 6, p. 36.

Anonymous. 1996b. Khahan "Dee" Kathoey Khaen Sao Meun Rak. *Chiang Mai News*, December 22, p. 1.

Anonymous 1997a. Mixed Opinions Obvious Reflection of Social Divisions. *The Nation*, January 29.

Anonymous. 1997b. Rajabhat Gay Ban Stirs Up Storm of Controversy. *The Nation*, January 26.

Barthes, R. 1977. *Image, Music, Text*. [ed. and trans. S. Heath]. New York: Hill and Wang.

Behar, R. 1993. *Translated Woman: Crossing the Border with Esperanza's Story*. Boston: Beacon Press.

Behar, R. and D. A. Gordon (eds.) 1995. *Women Writing Culture*. Berkeley: University of California Press.

Benjamin, W. 1968. *Illuminations*. New York: Schocken Books.

Besnier, N. 1994. Polynesian Gender Liminality Through Time and Space. In G. Herdt (ed.), *Third Sex, Third Gender: Beyond Sexual Dimorphism in Culture and History*. (pp. 285-328). New York: Zone Books.

Beyrer, C. 1998. *War in the Blood: Sex, Politics, and AIDS in Southeast Asia*. London, UK: Zed Books.

Blackwood, E. 2000. Culture and Women's Sexualities. *Journal of Social Issues* 56(2), 223-238.

Blackwood, E. and S. Wieringa (eds). 1999. *Female Desires: Same-Sex Relations and Transgender Practices Across Cultures*. New York: Columbia University Press.

Bock, C. 1985. *Temples and Elephants*. Bangkok: White Orchid Press.

Bornstein, K. 1994. *Gender Outlaw: On Men, Women and the Rest of Us*. New York: Routledge.

Brevard, A. 2001. *The Woman I was Not Born to Be: A Transsexual Journey*. Philadelphia: Temple University Press.

Brodkey, L. 1987. Writing Critical Ethnographic Narratives. *Anthropology and Education Quarterly* 18(1), 67-76.

Brummelhuis, H. T. 1999. Transformations of Transgender: The Case of the Thai *Kathoey*. In P. Jackson and G. Sullivan (eds.), *Lady Boys, Tom Boys, Rent Boys: Male and Female Homosexualities in Contemporary Thailand* (pp. 121-139). Binghamton, NY: The Haworth Press.

Caplan, P. 1997. *African Voices, African Lives: Personal Narratives from a Swahili Village*. New York: Routledge.

Chasnoff, S. 1996. Performing Teen Motherhood on Video: Authoethnography As Counterdiscourse. In S. Smith and J. Watson (eds.), *Getting a Life: Everyday Uses of Autobiography* (pp. 108-133). Minneapolis: University of Minnesota Press.

Clifford, J. and G. Marcus (eds.) 1986. *Writing Culture: The Poetics and Politics of Ethnography*. Berkeley: University of California Press.

Coleman, E., P. Cogan, and L. Gooren. 1992. Male cross-gender behaviour in Myanmar (Burma): A description of the Acault. *Archives of Sexual Behaviour* 21(3), 313-321.

Collins, P. H. 1990. *Black Feminist Thought: Knowledge, Consciousness, and the Politics of Empowerment*. New York: Routledge.

Costa, L. M. 2001. *Developing Identities: The Construction of Gender, Culture and Modernity in a Northern Thai Non-governmental Organization*. Doctoral dissertation, Department of Anthropology, University of Hawaii, Manoa.

Costa, L. M. and A. Matzner, 2002. Abusing Images: Domestic Violence in Thai Cartoon Books. *Intersections,* Issue 8. Available at http://wwwsshe.murdoch .edu.au/intersections/issue8/costa.html.

Cummings, J. 1997. *Thailand: A Lonely Planet Survival Kit*. Oakland, CA: Lonely Planet.

Darunee, T. and S. Pandey. 1987. The Status and Role of Thai Women in the Pre-Modern Period: A Historical and Cultural Perspective. *Sojourn* 2(1),125-49.

De Lind van Wijngaarden, J. W. 1995. A Social Geography of Male Homosexual Desire: Locations, Individuals and Networks in the Context of HIV/AIDS in Chiang Mai, Northern Thailand. Master's thesis, Department of Human Geography, University of Amsterdam.

De Lind van Wijngaarden, J. W. 1999. Between Money, Morality and Masculinity: Bar-Based Male Sex Work in Chiang Mai. In P. Jackson and G. Sullivan (eds.), *Lady Boys, Tom Boys, Rent Boys: Male and Female Homosexualities in Contemporary Thailand* (pp. 193-218). Binghamton, NY: The Haworth Press.

Devor, H. 1997. *FTM: Female-to-Male Transsexuals in Society*. Bloomington, IN: Indiana University Press.

East, J. 2000. Switch Hitters. *The Hollywood Reporter*, April 4, p. 8.

Elliston, D. 1995. Erotic Anthropology: "Ritualized Homosexuality" in Melanesia and Beyond. *American Ethnologist* 22(4), 848–867.

Freeman, J. M. 1978. *Untouchable: An Indian Life history*. London, UK: Allen and Unwin.

Freeman, J. M. 1979. Collecting the Life History of an Indian Untouchable. In S. Vatuk (ed.), *American Studies in the Anthropology of India*. New Delhi: Manohar.

Geertz, C. 1973. *The Interpretation of Cultures*. New York: Basic Books.

Ginsburg, F. D. 1989. *Contested Lives*. Berkeley: University of California Press.

Gluck, S. B. 1991. Advocacy Oral History: Palestinian Women in Resistance. In S. B. Gluck and D. Patai (eds.), *Women's Words: The Feminist Practice of Oral History* (pp. 205-219). New York: Routledge.

Gluck, S. B. and Patai D. 1991. *Women's Words: The Feminist Practice of Oral History*. New York: Routledge.

Gorman, M.R. 1998. *The Empress Is a Man: Stories from the Life and Times of Jose Sarria*. Binghamton, NY: Harrington Park Press.

Guillon, E. 1991. The Ultimate Origin of the World, or the Mula Muh, and Other Mon Beliefs. *Journal of the Siam Society* 79(1), 22-29.

Hale, A. 1984. The Search for a Jural Rule: Women in Southeast Asia—The Northern Thai Cults in Perspective. *Mankind* 14(4), 330-338.

Hale, A. 1979. A Reassessment of Northern Thai Matrilineages. *Mankind* 12, 138-150.

Hallett, H. 2000. *A Thousand Miles on an Elephant in the Shan States*. Bangkok: White Lotus Press.

Hammer, D. 1997. *Thai Scene 1998*. London, UK: Gay Men's Press.

Haraway, D. 1988. Situated Knowledges: The Science Question in Feminism and the Privilege of Partial Perspective. *Feminist Studies* 14(3), 575-599.

Harding, S. 1998. Subjectivity, Experience and Knowledge: An Epistemology from/for Rainbow Coalition Politics. In M. F. Rogers (ed.), *Contemporary Feminist Theory* (pp. 98-108). New York: McGraw Hill.

Herdt, G. 1997. *Same Sex, Different Cultures: Exploring Gay and Lesbian Lives*. Boulder, CO: Westview Press.

Horn, R. 2000. Sporty Little Number. *Time Magazine* (Asia Edition), March 27.

Irvine, W. 1982. *The Thai-Yuan "Madman," and the Modernizing, Developing Thai Nation as Bounded Entities Under Threat: A Study in the Replication of a Single Image*. Doctoral dissertation, University of London, United Kingdom.

Jackson, P. A. 1989. *Male Homosexuality in Thailand: An Interpretation of Contemporary Thai Sources*. New York: Global Academic Publishers.

Jackson, P. A. 1995a. *Dear Uncle Go: Male Homosexuality in Thailand*. Bangkok: Bua Luang Books.

Jackson, P. A. 1995b. Thai Buddhist Accounts of Male Homosexuality and AIDS in the 1980s. *The Australian Journal of Anthropology* 6(3), 140-153.

Jackson, P. A. 1997a. Kathoey><Gay><Man: The Historical Emergence of Gay Male Identity in Thailand. In L. Manderson and M. Jolly (eds), *Sites of Desire, Economies of Pleasure: Sexualities in Asia and the Pacific* (pp. 166-190). Chicago: University of Chicago Press.

Jackson, P. A. 1997b. Thai Research on Male Homosexuality and Transgenderism and the Cultural Limits of Foucaultian Analysis. *Journal of the History of Sexuality* 8(11), 52-85.

Jackson, P. A 1999a. An American Death in Bangkok: The Murder of Darrell Berrigan and the Hybrid Origins of *Gay* Identity in 1960s Thailand. *GLQ: A Journal of Lesbian and Gay Studies* 5(3), 361-411.

Jackson, P. A. 1999b. Same-Sex Sexual Experience in Thailand. In P. Jackson and G. Sullivan (eds.), *Lady Boys, Tom Boys, Rent Boys: Male and Female Homosexualities in Contemporary Thailand* (pp. 29-60). Binghamton, NY: The Haworth Press.

Jackson, P. A 1999c. Spurning Alphonso Lingis's Thai "Lust": The Perils of a Philosopher at Large. *Intersections: Gender, History, and Culture in the Asian Context* 2. Available at http://wwwsshe.murdoch.edu.au/intersections/issue2/jackson.html.

Jackson, P. A 1999d. Tolerant But Unaccepting: The Myth of a Thai "Gay Paradise." In P. Jackson and N. Cook (eds), *Genders and Sexualities in Modern Thailand* (pp. 226-242). Chiang Mai: Silkworm Books.

Jackson, P. A. 2000. An Explosion of Thai Identities: Global queering and re-imagining queer theory. *Culture, Health and Sexuality* 2(4), 405-424.

Jackson, P. and G. Sullivan (eds.). 1999. *Lady Boys, Tom Boys, Rent Boys: Male and Female Homosexualities in Contemporary Thailand*. Binghamton, NY: The Haworth Press.

Johnson, M. 1997. *Beauty and Power: Transgendering and Cultural Transformation in the Southern Philippines*. Oxford, UK: Berg.

Jorgensen, C. and S. Stryker. 2000. *Christine Jorgensen: A Personal Autobiography*. San Francisco: Cleis Press.

Kahn, J. 1998. Was That a Lady I Saw You Boxing? *The New York Times,* April 4, p. A4.

Keyes C. 1984. Mother or Mistress But Never a Monk: Buddhist Notions of Female Gender in Rural Thailand. *American Ethnologist* 11(2), 222-241.

Keyes C. 1986. Ambiguous Gender: Male Initiation in a Northern Thai Buddhist Society. In C. Walker Bynum, S. Harrell, and P. Richman (eds.), *Gender and Religion: On the Complexity of Symbols* (pp. 66-96). Boston: Beacon.

Kiratee Chanar. 1993. *Thang Sai Thii Saam*. Bangkok: Saam Sii Publishing.

Kluckhohn, C. 1945. A Navaho Personal Document with a Brief Paretian Analysis. *Southwestern Journal of Anthropology* 1, 260-283.

Knodel, J., C. Saengtienchai, M. Vanlandingham, and R. Lucas. 1999. Sexuality, Sexual Experience and the Good Spouse: Views of Married Thai Men and Women. In P. Jackson and N. Cook (eds.), *Genders & Sexualities in Modern Thailand* (pp. 78-92). Chiang Mai: Silkworm Books.

Kulick, D. 1997. The Gender of Brazilian Transgendered Prostitutes. *American Anthropologist* 99(3), 574-585.

Lang, S. 1999. Lesbians, Men-Women, and Two-Spirits: Homosexuality and Gender in Native American Cultures. In E. Blackwood and S.E. Wieringa (eds.), *Same-Sex Relations and Female Desires* (pp. 91-116). New York: Columbia University Press.

Langness, L. L. and G. Frank. 1985. *Lives: An Anthropological Approach to Biography*. Novato, CA: Chandler and Sharp Publishers, Inc.

Levy, R. 1971. The Community Function of Tahitian Male Transvestism: A Hypothesis. *Anthropology Quarterly* 44(1), 12-21.

Linde, C. 1993. *Life Stories: The Creation of Coherence*. New York: Oxford University Press.

Lyttleton, C. 2000. *Endangered Relations: Negotiating Sex and AIDS in Thailand*. Amsterdam: Harwood Academic Publishers.

Mandelbaum, D. G. 1973. The Study of Life History: Gandhi. Current Anthropology 14(3), 177-206.

Martino, M. 1977. *Emergence: A Transsexual Autobiography*. New York: Signet.

Mascia-Lees, F. E., P. Sharpe, and C.B. Cohen. 1989. The Postmodernist Turn in Anthropology: Cautions from a Feminist Perspective. *Signs* 15(1), 7-33.

Matzner, A. 2001a. The Complexities of Acceptance: Thai Student Attitudes toward *Kathoey*. *Crossroads* 15(2), 71-93.

Matzner, A. 2001b. *'O Au No Keia: Voices from Hawai'i's Mahu and Transgender Communities*. Philadelphia, PA: Xlibris Corporation.

Maytinee Bhongsavej and Suteera Thomson Vichitranonda. 2001. *Tunneling the Dead End: Gender Dimensions in Domestic Violence*. Bangkok: Gender and Development Research Instititute.

McCamish, M. 1999. The Friends Thou Hast: Support Systems for Male Commercial Sex Workers in Pattaya, Thailand. In P. Jackson and G. Sullivan (eds), *Lady Boys, Tom Boys, Rent Boys: Male and Female Homosexualities in Contemporary Thailand* (pp. 161-191). Binghamton, NY: The Haworth Press.

McCloskey, D. 2000. *Crossing: A Memoir*. Chicago: University of Chicago Press.

Menchu, R. and E. Burgos-Debray. 1984. *I, Rigoberta Menchu: An Indian Woman in Guatemala*. London, UK: Verso.

Mintz, S. 1974. *Worker in the Cane: A Puerto Rican Life History*. New York: W. W. Norton and Company.

Morris, R. 1994a. The Empress's New Clothes: Dressing and Redressing Modernity in Northern Thai Spirit Mediumship. In L. Milgram and P. Van Esterik (eds.), *The Transformative Power of Cloth in Southeast Asia* (pp. 53-74). Toronto: The Museum for Textiles and the Canadian Council for Southeast Asian Studies.

Morris, R. 1994b. Three Sexes and Four Sexualities: Redressing the Discourses on Gender and Sexuality in Contemporary Thailand. *Positions* 2(1), 15-43.

Morris, R. 2000. *In the Place of Origins: Modernity and Its Mediums in Northern Thailand*. Durham, NC: Duke University Press.

Muecke, M. 1992. Mother Sold Food, Daughter Sells Her Body: The Cultural Continuity of Prostitution. *Social Scientific Medicine* 35(7), 891-901.

Murray, T. F. 1992. Redirecting Sexual Orientation: Techniques and Justifications. *Journal of Sex Research* 29(4), 501-523.

Myerhoff, B. 1974. *Peyote Hunt: The Sacred Journey of the Huichol Indians.* Ithaca, NY: Cornell University Press.

Myerhoff, B. 1979. *Number Our Days.* New York: Dutton.

Nanda, S. 1999. *The Hijras of India: Neither Man Nor Woman,* Second Edition. Belmont, CA: Wadsworth Publishing.

Nanda, S. 2000. *Gender Diversity: Crosscultural Variations.* Prospect Heights, IL: Waveland Press.

Ochs, E. and L. Capps. 1996. Narrating the Self. *Annual Review of Anthropology* 25, 19-43.

O'Flaherty, W. D. 1980. *Women, Androgynes, and Other Mythical Beasts.* Chicago: The University of Chicago Press.

Ortner, S. 1996. *Making Gender: The Politics and Erotics of Culture.* Boston: Beacon Press.

Packard-Winkler, M. 1998. *Knowledge, Sex, and Marriage in Modern Bangkok: Cultural Negotiations in the Time of AIDS.* Doctoral dissertation in anthropology, The American University, Washington, DC.

Peacock, J. L. and D. C. Holland. 1993. Review Article: The Narrated Self: Life Stories in Process. *Ethos* 21(4), 367-383.

Peltier, A. 1991. *Pathamamulamuli: Tamnan Khao Phii Lanna [The Origin of the World in the Lan Na Tradition].* Chiang Mai: Suriwong.

Personal Narratives Group (eds). 1989. *Interpreting Women's Lives: Feminist Theory and Personal Narratives.* Bloomington, IN: University of Indiana Press.

Pettiway, L. 1996. *Honey, Honey, Miss Thang: Being Black, Gay, and on the Streets.* Philadelphia: Temple University Press.

Potter, S. 1977. *Family Life in a Northern Thai Village: A Study in the Structural Significance of Women.* Berkeley: University of California Press.

Prell, R. 1989. The Double Frame of Life History in the Work of Barbara Myerhoff. In The Personal Narratives Group (eds.), *Interpreting Women's Lives: Feminist Theory and Personal Narratives* (pp. 241-258). Bloomington, IN: Indiana University Press.

Rakkit Rattachumpoth. 1999. Foreword. In P. Jackson and G. Sullivan (eds.), *Lady Boys, Tom Boys, Rent Boys: Male and Female Homosexualities in Contemporary Thailand* (pp. xi-xviii). Binghamton, NY: The Haworth Press.

Rees, M. 1996. *Dear Sir or Madam: The Autobiography of a Female-to-Male Transsexual.* London, UK: Cassell.

Riessman, C. K. 1993. *Narrative Analysis.* Newbury Park, CA: Sage.

Rosaldo, R. 1989. *Culture and Truth: The Remaking of Social Analysis.* Boston: Beacon Press.

RuPaul. 1995. *Lettin' It All Hang Out: An Autobiography.* New York: Hyperion Press.

Scheper-Hughes, N. 1995. The Primacy of the Ethical: Propositions for a Militant Anthropology. *Current Anthropology* 36(3), 409-440.

Shostak, M. 1981. *Nisa: The Life and Words of a !Kung Woman*, New York: Vintage Books.

Sinnott, M. 1999. Masculinity and *Tom* Identity in Thailand. In P. Jackson and G. Sullivan (eds.), *Lady Boys, Tom Boys, Rent Boys: Male and Female Homosexualities in Contemporary Thailand* (pp. 97-119). Binghamton, NY: The Haworth Press.

Sinnott, M. 2000. The Semiotics of Transgendered Sexual Identity in the Thai Print Media: Imagery and the Sexual Other. *Culture, Health and Sexuality* 2(4), 425-440.

Sinnott, M. 2004. *Toms and Dees: Transgender Identity and Female Same-Sex Relationships in Thailand.* Honolulu: University of Hawaii Press.

Siraporn Nathalang 1997. Tai Creation Myths: Reflections of Tai Relations and Tai Cultures. *Tai Culture* 2(1), 56-66.

Sirikul Bunnag. 1997. Sukhavich Wants Special Centre for Homosexuals. *The Bangkok Post*, January 25.

Smith, P. 1997. Don't mess with the Iron Ladies. *National Enquirer*, April 22, p. 7.

Spiro, M. 1967. *Burmese Supernaturalism: A Study in the Explanation and Reduction of Suffering.* Englewood Cliffs, NJ: Prentice-Hall.

Stacey, J. 1988. Can there be a feminist ethnography? *Women's Studies International Forum* 11, 21-27.

Stewart, P.J. and A. Strathern (eds.) 2000. *Identity Work: Constructing Pacific Lives.* Pittsburgh, PA: University of Pittsburgh Press.

Storer, G. 1999a. Performing Sexual Identity: Naming and Resisting Gayness in Modern Thailand. *Intersections: Gender, History, and Culture in the Asian Context* 2. Available at http://wwwsshe.murdoch.edu.au/intersections/issue2/Storer.html.

Storer, G. 1999b. Rehearsing Gender and Sexuality in Modern Thailand: Masculinity and Male-Male Sex Behaviors. In P. Jackson and G. Sullivan (eds.), *Lady Boys, Tom Boys, Rent Boys: Male and Female Homosexualities in Contemporary Thailand* (pp. 141-159). Binghamton, NY: The Haworth Press.

Suteera Thomson Vichitranonda and Maytinee Bhongsavej. 2001. *Violence Against Women in Thailand: Development of Database and Indicators.* Bangkok: Gender and Development Research Institute.

Teh, Y.K. 1998. Understanding the Problems of *Mak Nyahs* (Male Transsexuals) in Malaysia. *South East Asia Research* 6(2), 165-180.

Thitsana Damrongsak. 2000. *Krathiam Rai Thiam Than.* Bangkok: Amarin Publishing.

Thongchai Winichakul 1994. *Siam Mapped: A History of the Geo-Body of a Nation.* Honolulu: University of Hawaii Press.

Thoonen, L. 2000. Life History and Female Initiation: A Case Study from Irian Jaya. In P.J. Stewart and A. Strathern (eds.), *Identity Work: Constructing Pacific Lives* (pp. 58-77). Pittsburgh, PA: University of Pittsburgh Press.

Took Took Thongthiraj. 1994. Toward a Struggle Against Invisibility: Love Between Women in Thailand. *Amerasian Journal* 20(1), 45-58.

Tsing, A. L. 1993. *In the Realm of the Diamond Queen*. Princeton, NJ: Princeton University Press.

Turton, A. 1972. Matrilineal Descent Groups and Spirit Cults of the Thai-Yuan in Northern Thailand. *Journal of the Siam Society* 60(2), 217-256.

Van Esterik, P. 1996. The Politics of Beauty in Thailand. In C.B. Cohen, R. Wilk, and B. Stoeltje (eds.), *Beauty Queens on the Global Stage: Gender, Contests, and Power* (pp. 203-216). New York: Routledge.

Van Esterik, P. 2000. *Materializing Thailand*. New York: Berg.

Voices of Thai Women (VTW). 1997. Domestic Violence in Thailand. *Voices of Thai Women* 15.

Von Mahlsdorf, C. 1995. *I Am My Own Woman: The Outlaw Life of Charlotte Von Mahlsdorf, Berlin's Most Distinguished Transvestite*. San Francisco: Cleis Press.

Wanida Kumanuwong. 1999. Reung jak pok [Interview with Sarat Rungreungwong]. *New Half Magazine*, February, pp. 3-5.

Warunee Fongkaew. 2002. Gender Socialization and Female Sexuality in Northern Thailand. In L. Manderson and P. Liamputtong (eds.), *Coming of Age in South and Southeast Asia: Youth, Courtship and Sexuality* (pp. 147-164). Richmond, UK: Curzon.

Watson, L.C. and M.B. Watson-Franke. 1985. *Interpreting Life Histories: An anthropological inquiry*. New Brunswick, NJ: Rutgers University Press.

Weinrich, J. and W. Williams. 1991. Strange Customs, Familiar Lives: Homosexualities in Other Cultures. In J. Gonsiorek and J. Weinrich (eds.), *Homosexuality: Research Implications for Public Policy* (pp. 44-59). London, UK: Sage Publications.

Weston, K. 1993. Lesbian/Gay Studies in the House of Anthropology. *Annual Review of Anthropology* 22, 339-367.

White, G. 1991. *Identity Through History*. Cambridge, UK: Cambridge University Press.

White, G. 2000. Afterword: Lives and Histories. In P. Steward and A. Strathern (eds.), *Identity Work: Constructing Pacific Lives* (pp. 172-187). Pittsburgh, PA: University of Pittsburgh Press.

White, G. and J. Kirkpatrick (eds.). 1985. *Person, Self, and Experience: Exploring Pacific Ethnopsychologies*. Berkeley: University of California Press.

White, H. 1981. The Value of Narrativity in the Representation of Reality. In W.J.T. Mitchell (ed.), *On Narrative* (pp. 1-23). Chicago: University of Chicago Press.

Whittaker, A. 2000. *Intimate Knowledge: Women and their Health in North-East Thailand*. St. Leonards, Australia: Allen and Unwin.

Whittaker, A. 2002. Water Serpents and Staying by the Fire: Markers of Maturity in a Northeast Thai Village. In L. Manderson and Pranee Liamputtong (eds.), *Coming of Age in South and Southeast Asia: Youth, Courtship and Sexuality* (pp. 17-41). Richmond, UK: Curzon.

Wijeyewardene, G. 1981. Scrubbing Scurf: Medium and Deity in Chiang Mai. *Mankind* 13(1), 1-14.

Wijeyewardene, G. 1986. *Place and Emotion in Northern Thai Ritual Behaviour.* Bangkok: Pandora.

Wilson, A. 2004. *The Intimate Economies of Bangkok: Tomboys, Tycoons, and Avon Ladies in the Global City.* Berkeley: The University of California Press.

Winter, S. 2002. Male, Female and Transgender: Stereotypes and Self in Thailand. *International Journal of Transgenderism* 6(1). Available at http://www.symposion.com/ijt/ijtvo06no01_04.htm.

Wood, W.A.R. 1991. *Consul in Paradise.* Bangkok: Trasvin Publications.

Woodward, A. 2002. My Story: Anatomically Incorrect. *Details,* May, 72-75.

Index

Male Bodies, Women's Souls
© 2007 by The Haworth Press, Inc. All rights reserved.
doi:10.1300/5750_08

Dear Customer:

Please fill out & return this form to receive special deals & publishing opportunities for you! These include:
- availability of new books in your local bookstore or online
- one-time prepublication discounts
- free or heavily discounted related titles
- free samples of related Haworth Press periodicals
- publishing opportunities in our periodicals or Book Division

❑ OK! Please keep me on your regular mailing list and/or e-mailing list for new announcements!

Name _____

Address_____

_____

*E-mail address _____

*Your e-mail address will never be rented, shared, exchanged, sold, or divested. You may "opt-out" at any time. May we use your e-mail address for confirmations and other types of information? ❑ Yes ❑ No

Special needs:
Describe below any special information you would like:
- Forthcoming professional/textbooks
- New popular books
- Publishing opportunities in academic periodicals
- Free samples of periodicals in my area(s)

Special needs/Special areas of interest:

_____

_____

_____

_____

Please contact me as soon as possible. I have a special requirement/project:

_____

_____

_____

PLEASE COMPLETE THE FORM ABOVE AND MAIL TO:
Donna Barnes, Marketing Dept., The Haworth Press, Inc.
10 Alice Street, Binghamton, NY 13904–1580 USA
Tel: 1–800–429–6784 • Outside US/Canada Tel: (607) 722–5857
Fax: 1–800–895–0582 • Outside US/Canada Fax: (607) 771–0012
E-mail: orders@HaworthPress.com

GBIC07

Visit our Web site: www.HaworthPress.com

STAPLE OR TAPE YOUR BUSINESS CARD HERE!